Exploring
the
Labyrinth

BROADWAY BOOKS
NEW YORK

Exploring the Labyrinth

A Guide for Healing and Spiritual Growth

MELISSA GAYLE WEST

PREFACE BY THE REVEREND DR. LAUREN ARTRESS
AUTHOR OF *WALKING A SACRED PATH*

BROADWAY

Broadway Books titles may be purchased for business or promotional use or for special sales. For information, please write to: Special Markets Department, Random House, Inc., 1540 Broadway, New York, NY 10036.

BROADWAY BOOKS and its logo, a letter B bisected on the diagonal, are trademarks of Broadway Books, a division of Random House, Inc.

Library of Congress Cataloging-in-Publication Data
West, Melissa Gayle.
    Exploring the labyrinth: a guide for healing and spiritual growth
       Melissa Gayle West. — 1st ed.
       p. cm.
    Includes bibliographical references and index.
    ISBN 0-7679-0356-0 (pbk.)
    1. Labyrinths—Religious aspects—Psychology. 2. Spiritual life.
    I. Title.
BL325.L3W47 2000   99-28662
291.3′7—dc21   CIP

FIRST EDITION

DESIGNED BY DEBORAH KERNER
ILLUSTRATIONS BY RICHARD WAXBERG

The illustration on page 8 is based on a
design by Robert Ferré.

10 9 8 7 6 5

To Gretchen,
book midwife extraordinaire,
for her dedication to the labyrinth

To Peter,
for introducing me to the labyrinth
and to She Who Knows,
always and forever at the Center

Acknowledgments

It takes one village to raise a child, they say, and I think no less is true for writing a book. I am deeply grateful for all the help and support I received during the writing of this book. This book has a multitude of parents, not one.

Thank you to Gretchen Schodde, my mother, Tibby Elebash, Alana Karran, Debra Jarvis, Jean Frinak, Barb Fischer, Alexandra Hart, Sharon Kaylen, Krista Heron, and Peter Wallis for their love and support during the transformative time of writing this book. Deep gratitude to my daughter, Elise, for allowing me the space to spread my wings; may I give you back that same gift, in love, many times over. Thanks to the wonderful staff at Harmony Hill for sheltering me and nourishing me, physically and emotionally, during the writing time: Gretchen Meyer, Maureen Kluver, Cindy Auwarter, Joe Hensley, and Fang.

Thanks to Harriet Bell: Your belief in my writing and your editing artistry brought me to a new level of the craft of writing.

Heartfelt thanks as well to my literary agent Sarah Jane Freyman and to that little voice that suggested she ask me in her gorgeous British accent one Sunday morning, "Melissa—have you ever heard of *labyrinths?*"

Thanks also to all those interviewed who gave generously of their time and wisdom as well as to all the workshop participants and clients who taught me about the labyrinth through their own experiences and stories.

Most of all, a deep bow in gratitude to the labyrinth and to the Spirit that forms its very matrix. May this book be a testimony to your power and love, and may it inspire others to know you.

Contents

Part Three
Playing and Healing
with the Labyrinth

Preface

It was Mother's Day, May 10, 1998 when the *New York Times* published a front-page article titled "Reviving Labyrinths: Paths to Inner Peace." There has been much publicity about labyrinths, but that article was the first to use the term "labyrinth movement." I immediately went to the *American Heritage Dictionary* to look up the word "movement." One definition said "the activities of a group of people to achieve a specific goal."

There is a labyrinth movement going on in the Western world, and the specific goal of this group, some of whom are named in these pages, is to reintroduce this ancient tool into modern-day consciousness. Melissa West's book *Exploring the Labyrinth* does a fine job taking on this task.

The labyrinth is receiving an amazing amount of attention, because walking the calming, circuitous path addresses many psychospiritual needs. The author identifies six areas of our lives where the labyrinth can be of help: "deepening spirituality, inwardness and connection to soul, access to intuition and creativity, simplicity, integration of body and spirit, and intimacy and community." Then, through her own experience and training, she expands and illuminates each area for the reader.

Melissa West is a psychotherapist whose experience with the labyrinth comes from her psychotherapeutic practice and from Harmony Hill, a holistic healing center for people confronted with life-threatening illnesses. She defines the labyrinth as an "archetypal map for the healing journey" and shares many stories that capture people's experiences.

When I began my work with the labyrinth in 1991, my life began to mysteriously unfold in new and surprising ways. Introducing the labyrinth at Grace Cathedral; creating Veriditas, The World-Wide Labyrinth Project; and writing *Walking a Sacred Path, the Rediscovery of the Labyrinth as a Spiritual Tool* all flowed out of my use of the labyrinth. I came to a high point during the writing when the focus of my work clarified in my mind: "Birth the creativity of the people." That is what the labyrinth does: It births people's creativity. Melissa West is a wonderful example of this vigorous and creative unfolding process.

You may know very little about labyrinths, or you may have walked them frequently enough to experience the transforming qualities of them. Either way, there are nuggets of wisdom in this book that will be helpful to everyone, but especially those who are sincerely committed to walking the Path.

The Reverend Dr. Lauren Artress
Canon for Special Ministries at Grace Cathedral
Founder of Veriditas, The World-Wide Labyrinth Project

Part One

Meeting the Labyrinth

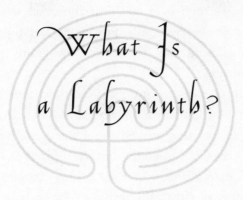

CHAPTER ONE

What Is a Labyrinth?

I flick on my computer, log on to the Internet, and type "labyrinth" into the waiting blank of my favorite search engine. After several seconds the screen informs me that 9,636 matches have been found: personal home pages on labyrinths; websites filled with stories and poetry about personal labyrinth experiences; web pages detailing labyrinth history and esoterica; churches and retreat center sites sporting pictures and stories about their labyrinths; organizations such Caerdroia and Veriditas (which reported 21,000 "hits" in a day following a *New York Times* story about the labyrinth renaissance) devoted exclusively to labyrinths; labyrinth online games; and even websites with virtual labyrinths to be walked with one's fingers for those without access to "real" labyrinths.

Labyrinths are also found on Earth as well as in cyberspace. They are being built on school playgrounds like Pinehurst in Seattle and the Cape Cod Lighthouse School in Orleans, Massachusetts, and on the campus of Ohio State University. The California Pacific Medical

Center in San Francisco offers its courtyard labyrinth to patients, family members, and hospital staff. Staff and patients who have used the labyrinth for stress reduction and contemplation have been so enthusiastic about their experiences that other hospitals around the country are building similar labyrinths. Prisons are building labyrinths on site or inviting facilitators to present programs with portable labyrinths to inmates.

Churches all over the country are creating labyrinths, from the huge Earth Wisdom Labyrinth on the grounds of a Unitarian church in Elgin, Illinois; to labyrinths at the United Methodist Community Church in Aspen, Colorado; and the Episcopal Church of the Redeemer in Mobile, Alabama; to the "mother church," Grace Cathedral in San Francisco, where the revival of the ecclesiastical labyrinth movement began. Private labyrinths are appearing in backyards and on the lawns of conference centers, on beaches, in snowfields, and deep in national forests; a recent *Boston Globe* article reported thirty labyrinths open to the public in the eastern part of Massachusetts alone.

Whoever you are, walking the labyrinth has something to offer you. If a creative or work project is challenging you, walking can get your creative juices flowing. When you are struggling with grief or anger or a physical challenge or illness, walking the labyrinth can point the way to healing and wholeness. If you're wanting a way to meditate or pray that engages your body as well as your soul, the labyrinth can be such a way. When you just want reflective time away from a busy life, the labyrinth can offer you time out. The labyrinth, as you will learn, holds up a mirror, reflecting back to us not only the light of our finest selves but also whatever restrains us from shining forth.

WHAT *IS* A LABYRINTH?

A labyrinth is different from a maze, though the two are often confused. The labyrinth is one of the oldest contemplative and transformational tools known to humankind, used for centuries for prayer, ritual, initiation, and personal and spiritual growth. This ancient and powerful tool is unicursal, offering only one route to the center and back out again: no blind alleys, dead ends, or tricks, as in a maze. No matter where you are in the labyrinth's coherent circuits you can always see the center. Once you set your foot upon its path, the labyrinth gently and faultlessly leads you to the center of both the labyrinth and yourself, no matter how many twists and turns you negotiate in the process.

Since the destination is assured, there are no obstacles to overcome, no muddles to figure out, no dead ends to retrace. What remains for the labyrinth walker is simply the deeply meditative and symbolic discipline of setting one foot in front of the other, of honoring the journey itself and what it has to teach. The mind can be stilled and attention paid to the body, the wisdom of the heart, and the graces of being rather than doing.

Remember the mazes on paper from childhood, tracing and retracing your pencil through a frustrating tangle of lines to get to the center? Mazes are puzzles: To figure one out, whether the maze is negotiated by foot or by pencil, the mind must be acutely focused in an active quest to find the right way out while avoiding getting hopelessly lost. Walking mazes, such as the formal boxwood hedge mazes in England, have walls or high hedges to obscure vision and confound the walker. They require acute attention to choices at intersecting paths and a high degree of critical awareness to remember detours and dead ends. Mazes do not grace those who enter; they taunt, tease, and challenge.

Two radically different scenes come to my mind when I think about the difference between a maze and a labyrinth: the Halloween maze at the Herb Farm near Seattle where I go to annually for an autumn outing with my family and a labyrinth walk I recently led for Winter Solstice.

Negotiating the Herb Farm's maze, set out in a field and constructed with eight-foot-high walls of hay bales, is challenging, confusing, and fun. Kids and grown-ups alike run through its twists and turns and dead ends, doubling back and bumping into one another while searching for the way out. Silliness and confusion reign amid much gleeful shouting when searchers finally escape the maze's challenging paths.

At the Winter Solstice labyrinth walk, deep and contemplative silence is the norm. Walkers slowly place one foot in front of the other on their journey to center, turned inward in meditation, healing work, or simple awareness of breath and step.

The labyrinth's ancient power derives from the fact that it is an archetypal map of the healing journey. The walk itself is a potent physical metaphor for the journeys of healing, spiritual and emotional growth, and transformation. In walking the labyrinth, we start at the perimeter. The path of the labyrinth, like any journey, has its own twists and turns, sometimes drawing near to and then away from the center.

It is only by keeping to the path, step by step, twist by turn, that one arrives at the physical center of the labyrinth, which signifies arriving at the center of our own lives and souls. Reaching the center of the labyrinth represents reaching the center, not only of our own hearts and spirits but of the goal we seek: Spirit, release from emotional or physical pain, a solution to a challenging problem or creative task, the unobstructed Self.

With today's labyrinth renaissance, two forms of the labyrinth have assumed prominence. These, the Cretan form and the Chartres form, are the ones explored in this book. Both produce the same powerful results; preferences are based on personal aesthetics, individual connection to liturgical forms or allegiance to Earth-based spiritualities, or simply the ease of installing one form over another.

The Cretan labyrinth, named after the island of Crete, home of the mythical labyrinth in which dwelled the Minotaur, takes the walker through seven circuits before reaching the center. It is the oldest and most universal form of the labyrinth, dating back at least 3,500 years. (See Figure 1.1.) Almost all other forms of the labyrinth are a variation of this classic model, save for the Chartres labyrinth.

The Chartres labyrinth, named after the permanent stone labyrinth set into the floor of Chartres Cathedral in France during the

FIGURE *1.1* CRETAN LABYRINTH

thirteenth century, has eleven concentric paths that wind through four quadrants of a circle. It is a distinctly Christian pattern, an equal-armed cross visible in its elegant layout. Set in the center is a rosette, a six-petaled design representing a rose, traditional symbol for the Virgin Mary. (See Figure 1.2.)

Why the astonishing and sudden popularity of the labyrinth? Walking the labyrinth fulfills six important contemporary needs: deepening spirituality; inwardness and connection to soul; access to intuition and creativity; simplicity; for integration of body and spirit; and intimacy

FIGURE 1.2 CHARTRES LABYRINTH

and community. The labyrinth addresses all of these six human needs, transforming the lives of those who take the time to walk its circuits.

DEEPENING SPIRITUALITY

We are a nation gripped by a powerful spiritual resurgence. Across the entire spectrum from mainstream religions to

Eastern philosophies to New Age movements, people in an increasingly driven and fragmented culture are searching for authentic spirituality and the sacred.

The labyrinth welcomes these seekers, opening its arms wide to anyone seeking authentic spiritual experience. The labyrinth is a powerful spiritual symbol that speaks to our souls in a way that transcends all creeds and beliefs. All spiritual traditions speak of life as a path, a spiritual journey, with its own twists and unexpected turns, to the heart of Spirit. Walking the labyrinth can help people step foot once again on their own paths, helping them to remember their own lives as spiritual journeys.

"The interest in the labyrinth is coming from every corner of society. You name it, I've probably heard something about it," says Jean Lutz, editor of the *Labyrinth Letter* and webmistress of one of the most comprehensive labyrinth websites in the world. "This widespread, across-the-board interest boggles my mind. People are so hungry for some handhold now to get spirituality into their lives in a concrete way. The labyrinth isn't just physical; it has a very powerful mystical quality. It's like the labyrinth is a kind of clue to existence, to the mysteries of life and Spirit. Just being in a labyrinth begins to bring some sense to all this mystery; it's like being on the Path, knowing that there are answers to all the Big Questions, even if I'll never know them."

Walking the labyrinth deepens one's spiritual path, whatever that path may be. The labyrinth can be a path of prayer, taking us—no matter whom or what we worship—to the center: the center of creation and the center of our own hearts and souls. The labyrinth welcomes us all with open arms, inviting us to walk directly with Spirit.

INWARDNESS AND CONNECTION TO SOUL

Stop for a moment. Take a deep breath. What are you feeling and knowing in your heart, your body, your soul, right now? When do you allow yourself to turn inward? How often do you get to unplug from TV, cell phone, to-do lists, computer, kids, partner, work?

For many of us, an uninterrupted turning within would be a delicious but impossible opportunity. We tell ourselves that we'll attend to our own needs when we get a month off; when the kids get older; or when we win the lottery. In the meantime we live our hurried lives from the outside in, responding to the pressures of work, home, and the impossible demands we put on ourselves.

The labyrinth offers us the great gift of making it easier to set aside the time and look inward. With each step we take we shed the outside world and slip more into our inner lives. During some walks, that inward movement may simply be about moving in deep silence and meditating in rich darkness. In others, tears or unexpected joy might be waiting in that inner space: a memory to walk through and heal; a vision of how our lives could be; a prayer we pray for our community and loved ones.

I encourage my psychotherapy clients to walk the labyrinth in my garden before our sessions to facilitate turning inward and leaving everyday pressures behind, and afterward to let the issues raised in the therapy sessions settle into their psyches before returning to homes or jobs.

"I come to therapy directly from work," says Robert, an attorney in a high-powered firm. "I spend the day working in a cutthroat corporate setting where I forget there's another way of treating others and myself. Walking the labyrinth before a session reminds me that I've got a soul, even if I have to shut it away to survive in my field. When I walk the labyrinth, I can take off all that battle armor and touch base inside.

"Walking the labyrinth, almost as much as therapy, has taught me that I walk different paths in different worlds—the outside world of my job and the inside world of my own soul. Becoming aware of those different paths, and of walking the labyrinth as a metaphor for my inward path, has helped me learn the importance of knowing which path I'm walking at any given time."

Like Robert, when we step into the labyrinth, we turn our backs on all the external hubbub that disconnects us from the riches of our own hearts and souls. Unplugged from the relentless demands of the world around us, we are free to look inside and renew the healing connection to our inner lives.

ACCESS TO INTUITION
AND CREATIVITY

By turning our attention inward we gain access to intuition and wisdom, inner sources of guidance that can give us invaluable feedback on questions and concerns we carry about our relationships, our work, our health and well-being, our spiritual lives.

"The labyrinth just naturally causes your attention to start turning inward, focusing in the present moment" says Neal Harris, originator of the giant stone Earth Wisdom Labyrinth in Elgin, Illinois. "Walking the labyrinth, it's so much easier to hear the intuitive messages. It's those intuitive messages that lead to our outward creativity."

During a labyrinth walk the left and right hemispheres of the brain are balanced, leading to the perfect state for accessing intuition and creativity. We let go of our typical linear and analytical ways of thinking and move into a more creative and intuitive awareness. Energy is freed up for seeking inner guidance for challenging issues; for looking at new perspectives on relationships; for inspiring creativity for work, projects, or hobbies. I have walked the labyrinth countless times for inspiration and new ideas in writing articles and books, for unjamming creative blocks, and for tapping into my own intuition for help in decision making and life-dreaming.

Many of the traditional methods for accessing creativity and intuition, such as creative visualization, journaling, and affirmations, can be combined with walking the labyrinth for even greater results, as you shall see in later chapters.

NEAL HARRIS

*The Earth Wisdom Labyrinth in Elgin, Illinois, is ninety-four feet in diameter
and uses twenty-five tons of stone.*

SIMPLICITY

We're all searching for simplicity in our lives," says Jean Lutz. "The labyrinth answers that need: It's so basic, so simple—it brings us back, always, to simplicity."

In our culture driven by experts who give us rules about the "right way" to do everything, from raising kids to communicating with spouses to organizing our lives, the labyrinth represents a refreshing return to the basics of walking and breathing and trusting the wisdom that lives deep within our hearts and souls.

"With my husband, it seems like there are so many rules for communicating effectively, the exact words and phrases you're supposed to say, that sometimes I lose sight of what it is that I'm really trying to say in the first place! I start feeling like the centipede trying so hard to make its feet go 'right' that it trips all over itself," one labyrinth walker told me. "When I walk the labyrinth, I can let go of all the dos and don'ts and just listen inside to what it is I really want to say to him. When I stop getting tangled up in all the rules and just let myself get 'simple,' I find what I most want to say and the best way for *me* to say it."

The labyrinth's gift is simplicity, both the simplicity of stripping away all external dos and don'ts to listen to our own voices and the simplicity of the walk itself. No advanced degrees are necessary to master the labyrinth, no long training sessions, no technical manuals. There are no "levels" to complete, nothing to memorize, no tests to take. All that is really required in walking the labyrinth is to show up, place one foot in front of the other, and breathe.

There is no "right way" to walk the labyrinth: In walking, we are thrown back on ourselves and our own experiences, instead having to measure our walk against some set of external standards or rules. In this simplicity, everything that takes place while walking becomes a mirror that allows us to look into our individual fears and anxieties.

"We all come to the labyrinth as ourselves—that's the great gift of that simplicity," says Lutz. "Don't let anyone else influence you about how walking the labyrinth is 'supposed' to be. You have to follow your own path. The labyrinth shows you that path."

INTEGRATION OF BODY AND SPIRIT

At the most basic level, walking the labyrinth restores our connection to our bodies, allowing us to shed stress and tension. Robert Ferré, the only production-labyrinth maker in the world, knows about labyrinths and also knows about the stresses of a challenging job. Ferré takes off for his backyard labyrinth when life's demands start taking their toll on his body and soul.

"When I walk my backyard labyrinth, I'm not accomplishing, not striving, not ticking things off my to-do list," says Ferré. "My body is trained now: I'll walk out the door and before I even get to the entrance of the labyrinth I start to relax because my body knows this is time out, it's time for me just to be with me. The labyrinth represents getting back to my own center, my own body, my own soul."

With this shedding of tension, the body can relax into sacred space. One of my favorite forms of meditation over the years has been Buddhist walking meditation. In this sort of meditation, I walk slowly and mindfully, feeling the placement of each foot on the ground. By the quiet awareness of breathing in and breathing out while mindfully taking each step, my body becomes a vehicle for the Sacred: My feet honor the earth and my own path; my breathing becomes the in-breath and outbreath of Spirit.

Walking the labyrinth is very similar to traditional walking meditations in Eastern traditions. Rather than transcending the physical world, as in many kinds of prayer and meditation, walking invites us to more fully inhabit our bodies, finding the presence of the Sacred in the immanence of our breathing and movement.

So much of the psychotherapeutic work I do with clients is to support them in reconnecting with the life flowing from their necks down: the life of the heart, the life of the gut, the life of the loins: our passions, fears, loves, all the ways that our souls speak through our bodies. As long as we live from the neck up, we are cut off from our kinesthetic wisdom. Walking the labyrinth opens us to the passionate life and wisdom we carry, always, in our bodies.

INTIMACY AND COMMUNITY

Mary Ellen Johnson, a Unity lay minister certified by Veriditas at Grace Cathedral in San Francisco as a labyrinth facilitator, remembers when walking the labyrinth healed a strained friendship. Mary Ellen and Stephanie couldn't see eye to eye on some painful personal issues, and their close relationship had become distant and conflicted. One evening they walked the labyrinth together, searching for a way to rebuild the intimacy that had meant so much to both.

"We couldn't talk about the issues anymore—they were just too painful," Mary Ellen recalls. "What happened while we were walking the labyrinth was that we both realized we couldn't solve our difficulties with our minds—there were just too many pieces of the puzzle missing. We let go of trying to figure it out and understand it and fix it.

"Walking the labyrinth let us settle into our hearts; we both could just allow the difficulty to be. As we talked afterward, there was this sense that okay, there was this shared pain, but it was really time to let it heal and just get on with life and our relationship. The labyrinth reminded us to open our hearts, just continue to walk the path toward the center, so to speak, rather than getting stuck in one of the turns."

After facilitating many group walks, Mary Ellen has found that people learn powerful lessons about relationships in the labyrinth. "When you walk through a labyrinth with people, you temporarily go off toward different quadrants, and then come in closer, like times when you're walking in agreement and closeness, so to speak, with one another, but then hit conflict or distance. The beauty of the labyrinth is that everyone is on the same path, but we're at different places on the path as we all move toward the center. We walk together, we move apart, but in the big picture we are all walking toward the center. Relationships that have depth and longevity do the very same thing, and the labyrinth is such a powerful concrete reminder of that."

I learn a great deal when I lead retreats based on labyrinth walking at Harmony Hill, a center where I serve as program and cancer retreat coordinator. Walking the labyrinth is a core of all the workshops, no matter what the specific content: finding balance, menopause, life transitions, healing from cancer, seasonal celebrations.

I have been deeply moved by how the labyrinth has taught cancer patients about wholeness, church congregations and board members of nonprofits about community, mourners about the healing of the heart, long-estranged family members about reconciliation. When walking the labyrinth we all—no matter how different our lives may be—become pilgrims together on the path to wholeness.

Throughout this book you will read stories of men and women who have walked the labyrinth for spiritual, emotional, and physical healing, fostering of creativity, and intimacy with self and others. In addition, you will receive practical information on how to build several kinds of labyrinths and how to work with them in an astonishing variety of ways that will enhance your life and improve your well-being.

This book is in three parts:

- PART ONE shows you why the labyrinth has such astonishing contemporary appeal. It introduces you to walking, and working with, the labyrinth, and gives you some of its history so that you may better understand its power.
- PART TWO teaches you to construct temporary or permanent indoor and outdoor labyrinths from a wide variety of materials, explains how to prepare the labyrinth space for walking, tend the labyrinth as a meditative discipline, and create labyrinth altars.
- PART THREE gives you specific ways to use the labyrinth for spiritual growth, healing work, creativity enhancement, goal setting, and ritual and celebration.

All of these chapters, all of their suggestions and exercises, are only turns in the path. What I hope for you is that whichever ones you choose will lead, like the labyrinth's circuits, to the center: more love, more grace, more Spirit to support and guide your own path in life, wherever that path may lead.

Come with me now. Let us begin the journey.

CHAPTER TWO

Walking the Walk

I write this chapter on a summer afternoon in the cool dappled shade of a huge cedar near my favorite labyrinth at Harmony Hill, a retreat center on Hood Canal about two hours from my Seattle home. I'm here this weekend as a writer for personal writing time rather than in my usual role as program coordinator or retreat leader.

A meditation retreat is beginning this afternoon, and as people arrive they head to the labyrinth for a walk before the program begins. I watch people as I write, observing how each person uniquely approaches, and walks, the labyrinth.

The retreat leader shows up barefoot in the heat. He pauses a moment in thought or prayer at the labyrinth entrance, then walks slowly and reflectively to the center. Once there he sits down on a small bench, his back resting against the redwood tree growing in the center. Although his eyes are open, his gaze is obviously turned inward.

A middle-aged woman heads energetically into the labyrinth without pausing at the entrance, taking the circuits in great deliberate

A Chartres labyrinth with a redwood tree in the center, Harmony Hill, Washington.

strides. Once at the center, though, she stops and closes her eyes. Her face and body soften and relax. Going out her gait is slower; I watch her stop and gaze at the marigolds and loosestrife blooming around the perimeter of the labyrinth.

A tall man in his twenties wearing a Mickey Mouse T-shirt lopes up to the labyrinth. At the entrance he cocks his head to one side briefly, peers up into the branches of the redwood, shrugs his shoulders, and steps in as if beginning an adventure. When almost to the center, he breaks into a great grin that keeps returning to light up his face all the way through the rest of the walk.

I am amazed, once again, at how accurately our individual personalities, and our states of mind and heart, are reflected in the way we actually walk the labyrinth.

MY OWN WALK

My first labyrinth walk, in a temporary rope labyrinth at a weekend workshop, was uneventful. I secretly wondered if I was walking the labyrinth correctly, figuring that if I did it "right" some astounding revelation would shake me to my core. It didn't happen.

I envied others their powerful experiences in the labyrinth, including my friend Debra who had life-changing insights the first time she walked. My first walks reminded me of my first awkward attempts at meditation when it seemed as if all I did was try to figure out if I was meditating correctly.

Looking back on those early walks, I know now that I was simply trying too hard. Instead of allowing the labyrinth to teach and lead me, I was struggling to do it "right." I tried harder and harder each walk to get "it," not knowing what "it" was, but knowing I was missing something, feeling increasingly frustrated.

An invitation to build a backyard labyrinth for friends proved to be the first meaningful step in my own labyrinth journey. One fall weekend we hauled river rocks into the ancient spiral pattern of the labyrinth, laying down moss between the smooth gray stones. By Sunday evening we had created a seven-circuit Cretan labyrinth that seemed to emerge softly from the earth. We placed luminarias—candles set in sand inside small paper bags—around the labyrinth.

Worn out from two days of lifting stones, I decided to enjoy the view from the deck while others initiated the labyrinth with a first walk. Later when all was quiet in the garden, I stepped into the labyrinth and began walking quickly. How fast can I do this, I wondered, so I can finish and get back to the celebration potluck?

I stumbled and fell. Brushing dirt off my palms, I tried to figure out what circuit I had been walking, and in which direction. How was I going to do it right if I didn't even know where I was going?

Panicking, and rushing more than ever to finish, I strode purposefully toward what I hoped was the center.

I soon found myself back at the entrance instead.

Well, I thought, I could quit now, pretend I walked the whole thing and get back to the party. Berating myself for my hasty carelessness, I turned away from the labyrinth toward the bright lights of the house.

Wait, a voice said inside me, *isn't this how you do a whole lot of your life?*

I stopped and looked back.

The labyrinth was waiting quietly for me. I took a deep breath and wondered, How many events in my life have I power-walked through, in a hurry to get to the next event, which I then power-walked through in a hurry to get to the next event? How many times have I bluffed and pretended to know exactly what I was doing and where I was going, when I really didn't have a clue?

Okay, said that same voice, *are you going to do all that again? Or are you going to make a different choice this time?*

I stepped back into the labyrinth. Walking into the darkness, I felt the spongy moss yielding under each step. My breathing slowed and softened, my shoulders dropped, as I mindfully navigated each circuit by the soft glow of the luminarias.

I realized there was no "right way" to walk this path. I didn't have to pretend to know exactly where I was going and what I was doing in the labyrinth, as I did in so much of the rest of my life: If I took the path step by step by step, I would reach the center. Even if I "messed up" and got lost again, I'd know because I would simply end up at the entrance. Everything was all right.

I arrived in the center and sat down on the cool moss.

Watching the flame of the candle next to me, I realized that this walk had taught me some powerful lessons about how I walked the path of my own life. I understood that the way I had attempted initially to walk was the same way I bluffed my way through a lot of my life. These labyrinth lessons weren't just easy head knowledge, the kind at which I was so proficient. They were, that night, foot knowledge, breath knowledge, heart knowledge.

I walked out mindfully, bowed in gratitude to the labyrinth as a new teacher and friend, and joined my friends in celebration.

During your first walk, you may have an insightful and life-changing experience. You are at least as likely to have another sort of experience: one of deep thoughtfulness or simply a quiet awareness of the present moment. You may wonder, just as I did, if you are doing it "right."

What I can assure you—based on both my own personal experience and facilitating many walks for others—is that all your experiences in the labyrinth will be right. The labyrinth offers us a wide range of experiences, ranging from intense and dramatic to quiet and outwardly uneventful. All are valuable, and all can be learning experiences.

THE GIFT OF OUR OWN RHYTHMS

The labyrinth provides a marvelous opportunity to recover the rhythms of our own breath, our own gait, the innate ebb and flow of our own thoughts and feelings. Since there is no "right way" to walk the labyrinth, we are free to discover our own way to walk each time we step foot into its circuits.

I have seen people saunter, run, dance, crawl, hop, skip, twirl, and shuffle along the path. You may find yourself starting at one pace and then, as you settle into the walk, shifting into a faster or slower gait, or another sort of walk altogether. You may enter one way and exit another.

Walking the labyrinth is an opportunity to drop your constricted, time-bound self and move to the music of your own soul. Once you recover your own rhythm, you many find that your body wishes to move and express itself in new ways.

I found that during a time of great personal and professional change—much to my chagrin!—my arms wanted to spread wide as I walked the labyrinth. I felt foolish about doing so, even when I was walking the labyrinth alone, and resisted the movement for several walks. I finally realized my pride was silly and useless, and sheepishly spread my arms during an evening walk. To my astonishment I felt as if I were unfurling a magnificent set of wings for the first time.

Then (after furtively looking around—I still wasn't quite comfortable) I stretched my arms wider, opening my chest to the fierce freedom of a great raptor about to take flight. Releasing my embarrassment, I soared through the circuits, exulting in the growing strength of my wings.

I needed to "fly" the labyrinth frequently for several months as I discovered a new freedom and power in my life. When I felt comfortable enough, I allowed myself to spread my arms when walking with others and learned a valuable lesson: that I was my own worst judge and jury. No one looked at me askance or clucked their tongues when I opened my arms. I discovered that just as I was the only one judging myself for being foolish, I was also the only one who could give myself permission to fly.

Finding, as I did, that we are free to stretch and try new ways of being in the labyrinth without being judged by others can be one of the labyrinth's greatest gifts. Neal Harris, a counselor who built the massive Earth Wisdom Labyrinth in Elgin, Illinois, calls the labyrinth the "playground of the spirit." "There's so much dogma about correct ways to use the labyrinth," says Harris. "I like to tell people that anything goes." Harris likes to tell about his first experience in the labyrinth to illustrate. "After the walk, when I was sitting by the side of the labyrinth waiting for others to finish the walk, I got this funny idea: 'What if I stood on my head?' My first thought was 'Oh, you're just going to embarrass the heck out of yourself. Why would you even consider it?' But I stood on my head, and it led to a profound perception, watching other walkers on the ceiling with this labyrinth. It reminded me of floating butterflies.

"That's when I realized that to receive the body wisdom that can flow up during this mind-body-spirit experience of walking the labyrinth, it's incredibly important to honor what you're led to do. You never know what's going to bubble up, and you never know what's going to further your own evolution. You can't decide beforehand what's going to be best for your own healing process when you walk the labyrinth."

Most people didn't even notice that Harris stood on his head. "That's the kicker, that remnant of adolescence when you're sure everyone's watching you, but they're really involved in their own stuff. I love to pass that story on to people and tell them that 'step on a crack, break your mother's back' does not apply to walking the labyrinth."

LABYRINTH AS JOURNEY

The labyrinth has always represented journey: the journey through life, death and rebirth, the spiritual journey, the initiatory journey. The labyrinth still speaks to us today as a powerful symbol of journeying.

That journey can be your whole life. It can also represent a particular journey in your present or past life: school, a relationship, a creative project. It can be fun, and instructive, to walk consciously with a specific journey in mind to reflect upon, but often the labyrinth itself will reveal the particular journey and teach you how to be a journeyer.

I had a client who discovered to her dismay that her mind repeated "What's the use? It's hopeless . . . " when she walked my backyard labyrinth for the first time. Elaine realized that her resigned attitude was the way she approached her whole life. "When I was walking, it was like I was moving metaphorically through sludge, lots of deep, endless amounts of it. That sludge seemed to go on forever. I realized I approached so much of my life that way—my teaching job, housework, stuff with my husband, you name it. Thick, dark yuck, all of it, and me wondering why I even bothered.

"Well, the surprise for me in the labyrinth was that when I picked my head up from all the sludge I was walking through and feeling so hopeless about, I could see the center! It was right there all along, but I had my face down in all that muck and so I couldn't notice it.

"When I realized the center was right there, my whole mood shifted. All that imaginary sludge I was walking through lost its power. I saw that I had the choice to get mired down in it or just walk through it knowing I was heading for the center. What a victory it was to get to the center! I felt like dancing on the way out. All that sludge in my life lost its power over me.

"In fact—I thought about this a lot the next week—I realized that a lot of what I had labeled sludge in my life really wasn't sludge at all, it's just that I was so conditioned to see everything as a struggle that I couldn't see it any other way. Even when challenges came up that week—my kids in the classroom having a wild day or the starter going out on my car—I could remember it was just part of the journey, that I could walk through it with my head up, knowing that center was always there."

As you work with the labyrinth you may find that it invites you, as it did me, to try new gaits, new movements, new dances with your own life. The more you can allow yourself to say yes to this invitation to dance in a new way within the labyrinth, the more you will find yourself hearing the same new music everywhere, inviting you to dance new and exciting steps in your relationships, your work, your creative life.

SOLO JOURNEY

Remember my story about being in such a hurry to "get there" that I was never in the present? How the labyrinth gently reminded me of my "hurry sickness" and invited me to try something else?

I was always the kid on the family vacation who wanted to know if we were there yet two blocks after pulling out of the driveway. I have spent a painfully large amount of time still in the backseat, fidgeting and squirming and knowing life didn't really start until I got "there," though "there" has appeared in thousands of guises in my journey: college, marriage, career, children, success, vacations . . .

The labyrinth, ever since that evening walk, has remained a loving teacher to me about the value of the journey itself, of honoring the process rather than straining for the goal. I walk when working on a writing project, to remind me to relax and take the writing one page (sometimes, one sentence!) at a time. I walk when I feel challenged by my adolescent daughter, the labyrinth reminding me to stop and embrace the many joys our relationship has to offer me right now, rather than worrying about how we're ever going to get to the other side. The labyrinth keeps reminding me that if I stay fixated on that ever-changing "there" I miss out on the sweet and enduring graces of the present moment, of life unfolding around and within me.

The labyrinth can also reveal to us when we walk solo the buried glory of our best and truest selves. During one labyrinth workshop David, burned out by office politics in his public relations firm, discovered how much bigger he was than he gave himself credit for. "I was feeling angrier and angrier, tighter and tighter with the power struggles and jockeying happening every day with the downsizing. I looked around the firm at all the other guys acting like jerks and realized that I was doing exactly the same thing. Trouble was, I couldn't see any way out of it. Do you know how awful it is every morning to wake up and discover you're the same jerk that went to bed the night before? It was like being in a really bad dream I couldn't wake up from."

David came to the workshop feeling hopeless about finding any way out of his mess. He walked the labyrinth with the intention of being shown a different way to be with the office situation. "Nothing much happened at first," he recalled later. "I was just walking and walking, determined to make something happen. All of a sudden some bird's song brought me to. I realized I was completely caught up, again, in the whole office drama, and not seeing a damn thing around me. I stopped and looked around, saw the trees, heard that bird again. I realized what a narrow band of life I was seeing when I got caught up in the struggles.

"Then—this was the real kicker—I started walking again and realized how much I was missing out on me! It was like I was identifying myself with one tiny little turn in my work path and forgetting that's all it was—a tiny little turn. When I saw myself as that turn, I lost sight of all of me—just like I lost sight of the whole labyrinth. I'm a whole lot more than office struggles, just like the labyrinth is a whole lot bigger than any of its turns."

David grinned as he remembered what happened next. "I had to stop again, because I was so blown away by my next thought. 'Wow!' I thought. 'I'm just like the labyrinth. I've got lots of twists and turns, but I've got a center, too. I can be all of that—the twists and turns, but I am also the center, and the outside, both of which are a whole lot bigger than the path itself.'"

David realized with relief that he could bring his "big self," as he put it, to his job: his integrity, his connection to God, his understanding that office politics were not the Big Picture. When acting from that "big self" he had many options, including compassion for both himself and the other people caught up in the power struggle, simply not available when functioning out of a smaller, tighter self. David returned to work on Monday with a picture of the labyrinth in hand to put on his desk, "to remind me of who I really am."

WALKING WITH OTHERS

When you're walking the labyrinth with others, a powerful mirror is held up before you that basically shows you how productive or unproductive are the attitudes, thoughts, belief systems, and behaviors that you carry in everyday life," says Neal Harris. "It becomes a very powerful opportunity for personal transformation. You can look at these judgments and the belief systems they represent as you walk: 'Oh, this person ahead of me is going way too slow. I'm so frustrated, I wish they'd get out of my way,' instead of simply walking around them. You then realize, Gee, I do this same thing when I'm out walking the street. Someone is walking in front of me, too slow for me, but I end up just walking at their pace and not mine. That's not helpful for me anymore. Maybe that was productive a long time ago when I was trying to learn to be polite, but is it still productive for me now to do that?"

Harris witnesses people experiencing transformation as a result of seeing their own belief systems show up as they walk with others. "You get hit in the head with that stuff in the labyrinth—it's been such a huge help in showing me the error of my ways, how I still carry old and outdated ways of being with others."

The labyrinth can not only show us ourselves, but it can lead us into deeper relationship with others, whether we walk with intimate others or total strangers. When we can understand the people we walk with to be sharing the same basic journey through life, with all its twists and turns, we can be freed to respect and love others just as they are in their path.

Debra Jarvis, a hospice chaplain friend of mine, likens walking the labyrinth with others to gaining a bird's-eye view of relationships. Debra was moved by the very different perspective she gained on relationships while walking. "You know, so often I see others only from my own limited perspective. It's so easy for me to judge them according to my own criteria about how 'spiritual' they are, or where they are on their life journey.

"When I walk the labyrinth, I am reminded that I don't have the whole picture, the bird's-eye view, the God's-eye view. Being with others in the labyrinth removes all that judgment—I can see we're all on the same path, just at different places. Just because someone seems closer to, or farther from, the center than me doesn't mean it's necessarily so; that's just my perspective on that particular circuit. Walking the labyrinth reminds me we're all on the same path, no matter how it seems to my own very limited perspective."

I remember one particularly powerful walk with my friend Peter and several other close friends. Peter and I had met for dinner with Jaimie and her daughter Kyna, for whom I was planning a menarche ritual to be celebrated later that weekend. The four of us decided to go to an open labyrinth walk together.

Walking by candlelight in the church with the three of them—a young girl on the threshold of womanhood, her mother in the full flower of her maturity, myself in the beginning of perimenopause, and Peter entering elderhood—I wept for the poignant passage of time.

Here we all are, I thought as I walked, moving through our lives together. I brushed Peter's hand when we passed on neighboring circuits, overwhelmed at the unbelievable preciousness of relationships in the face of our own mortality.

When walking the labyrinth to deepen relationships, the "other" need not even be present physically. Renee Gibbons, a writer and performer of a one-woman show on breast cancer, experienced the healing of a long-standing painful relationship with her sister who lived a continent away. One morning Renee "happened" upon the labyrinth in Grace Cathedral in San Francisco and, knowing nothing about the labyrinth, decided to walk it.

When Renee, a self-styled "militant atheist" since age thirteen, reached the center she heard a voice say "Send an angel to your sister Fiona." Renee was deeply angry at Fiona and hadn't talked to her in several years. Unsettled by the communication, Renee stopped in the cathedral gift shop to ask for directions to the bathroom.

"When I went in," Renee remembers, "my eyes went straight to this book—it just popped out at me. I opened it up at random, to a big picture of an angel. I read the frontispiece to the book and it explained that these were illustrations from Morse melodies. These melodies were songs we had sung as a family growing up in Ireland. I was hooked; there was real power in what happened in the labyrinth and now this. I bought the book. I thought, how am I going to send this to my sister? I don't want to endorse her mistreatment of me. But I thought, I'm obviously supposed to send it to her. I just wrote inside, 'Ever your sister,' and mailed it to her. I was so relieved.

"A lot of the bitterness and bad feelings I had toward her just dissipated with the labyrinth walk and the sending of the book. It was a huge relief, and a huge healing of a very old wound. We are now back in relationship, something I didn't think was ever going to happen."

ANNETTE REYNOLDS

WALKING INTO COMMUNITY

Walking the labyrinth doesn't just deepen intimacy with family and friends, however. It can be a powerful catalyst for opening to others we know little or not at all. I use the labyrinths in as many workshops as I can. Walking the labyrinth can build community quickly even in a group of strangers, cutting through the resistances to intimacy we all carry through the opening of the heart on a shared journey.

Mary Ellen Johnson recalls the life-changing walk of a woman in one of her labyrinth workshops. "I worked once with an older black lesbian who walked the labyrinth with a lot of people she didn't know. In the sharing afterward she said, 'My life has been about hating people who were prejudiced against me. I realized in the labyrinth we're all on the same path. Maybe I ought to not assume that people will be prejudiced against me and instead focus on the commonalities we share as human beings.'

"I was thinking, that's big stuff—she has three of the biggies that people can be prejudiced against, and after that walk she realized she could be a catalyst for change and healing rather than be aware of differences and division. It's so true that once you walk the labyrinth with a group of people they can never be strangers to you again; there is something about walking with others that lets you see them as real people, without all the projections we lay upon them."

I, too, had a life-changing walk where I learned how labels hinder community. I once attended a weekend workshop that the Reverend Dr. Lauren Artress, whose groundbreaking work with the labyrinth I greatly respect, gave at a cathedral where I had previously served on staff for many years as a psychotherapist. I walked into the cathedral on Friday evening and discovered, to my chagrin, that many in the audience were former as well as current clients.

What started out as a mildly uncomfortable situation for me (and, I know, for them) turned into a powerful experience. As we traveled the labyrinth together, walk after walk, I moved through my initial discomfort and came to understand with my heart and soul how we were all fellow travelers on the same healing journey. The labels of "therapist" and "client" fell away in the labyrinth's turns. Sharing the center with them, I could know each one not as "my client" but in the full glory of his or her humanness and sacredness; I myself could share wounds and glories not as "therapist" but as woman and human being.

Those walks deeply affected me personally as well as vocationally as a psychotherapist. That weekend still reminds me that we are not whatever labels happen to be sticking to us at any given time: client, therapist, parent, teacher, artist, attorney. That weekend the labyrinth taught me, at a level far deeper than my conscious mind, that we are all pilgrims walking our own singular walks on the same sacred path.

CHAPTER THREE

The Power of the Labyrinth

To understand the labyrinth's gifts, it helps to be aware of what labyrinths have meant in the centuries before our own and how the labyrinth itself embodies sacred space.

Imagine Sardinia, 3,500 years ago. You are a mourner in a funeral procession, winding deep into the stone cavern of a burial chamber. Torches flicker in the tomb, throwing into high relief a petroglyph of a labyrinth. As the burial ceremony begins you study the labyrinth for comfort in your grief, knowing it offers a map for death and rebirth for your deceased friend. This labyrinth shows you the circuitous route that your friend will follow into the tomb of Mother Earth. Your eyes rest for a moment at the center, knowing that this center will transform from tomb to womb, birthing your friend into her new life in the spirit realms back via the same winding route.

Imagine Arizona, 1,000 years ago. You are an Anasazi Indian, living high in the cliff dwelling of Casa Grande. It is a cold afternoon in January, too cold to venture from the mesa, and you idly scratch a

Walking the Chartres labyrinth at Chartres Cathedral, France.

crude labyrinth into the adobe walls of your pueblo. As you carve out
the labyrinth from the soft pink earth, you remember how this
labyrinth represents your people's emergence into this world from the
previous world in which they dwelt. Your spirit swells with pride as
your fingers trace your people's birth from the center of this labyrinth.

Imagine France, 800 years ago. You are in Chartres Cathedral
near Paris. In this great vaulting cathedral you pause at the entrance
to the stone labyrinth, recently inlaid so carefully into the floor of the
nave. Looking up at the jewel-colored light streaming through the
rose window high in front of you, you ask God to bless your journey
into the center of the labyrinth. You have prepared for this journey for
months with prayer. This walk represents the dream of a lifetime:
Instead of making the pilgrimage to Jerusalem, too far and too dangerous, you walk this labyrinth now. You are on holy ground.

The labyrinth, with its circumambulation of and eventual arrival at
the center through a single path, seems to have evolved from an
archetypal symbol known in virtually every culture throughout time:
the spiral, the universal symbol of growth and transformation.

FIGURE 3.1 SPIRAL

THE MAGIC OF SPIRALS

Stop for a moment and place the index finger from your nondominant hand at the entrance to the spiral shown in Figure 3.1. Take a deep breath, and slowly trace the spiral inward toward the center. Imagine that you are moving from the rim of creation to its very center. Let your finger rest a moment in the center. Take another deep breath and trace the spiral out, imagining this time that you are moving out into the physical manifestation of spirit through creation.

The spiral is literally encoded into the universe; it is a map for the growth and transformational processes of life itself. The world around us spirals in the scalar patterns of a pinecone, the glistening chambers of a nautilus shell, the vortex of water spinning down a drain. Our own bodies spiral: Trace the whorl of hair at the crown of your head, the point of contact with the divine in spiritual traditions the world over. We carry spirals from the winding code of our DNA to the cochlea of our inner ear to the whorls on our fingertips, those spirals whose imprints are uniquely our own.

Spirals—inscribed in stone the world over since Megalithic times—serve as threshold markers at holy sites in China, Egypt, Siberia, Europe, Mexico. These graven spirals delineate the boundary between secular and sacred in temples and burial sites, marking a person's passage from—or death to—the everyday world and rebirth into the realm of the sacred by entering hallowed ground. Humankind invokes Spirit by moving in spirals. Sufi Dervishes whirl in ecstatic dance, spiraling the universe into being. Half a world away, young women of the South African Bavenda tribe perform the Python dance, spiraling around the old women of their tribe to invoke fertility and cosmic harmony.

According to psychoanalyst Carl Jung in *Archetypes and the Collective Unconscious*, the process of healing and individuation most resembles the dynamic of a spiral: "We can hardly help feeling that the unconscious moves spiralwise around a center gradually getting closer, while the characteristics of the center grow more and more distinct."

SPIRAL INTO LABYRINTH

This spiraling journey to a center is the transformational movement humankind has forever traced in the labyrinth. "The spiral or labyrinth depicted in ancient tombs," notes Jill Purce in *The Mystic Spiral*, "implies a death and reentry into the womb of the earth, necessary before the spirit can be reborn into the land of the dead. But death and rebirth also mean the continuous transformation and purification of the spirit throughout life."

The earliest known labyrinth is that mentioned at the beginning of this chapter, a petroglyph on the wall of a subterranean stone burial chamber in Sardinia called *Tomba del Labarinto*, or Tomb of the Labyrinth. Petroglyphs and drawings of labyrinths from the second millennium B.C. have been found in India, Greece, Syria, and Italy. Roman labyrinths—nearly sixty of them—have been uncovered throughout the former Roman Empire, from Britain to Spain to Yugoslavia to North Africa.

Labyrinths appeared throughout the world in the thousand years from A.D. 500 to A.D. 1500. Great stone labyrinths were built along the Scandinavian coastline from Iceland to Russia. Labyrinths were drawn and carved into cliff dwellings and mesas in the American Southwest. Turf labyrinths—made by cutting trenches into turf for the paths, with turf ridges delineating the path—were cut into the earth in Germany, Poland, and England. Stone and tile labyrinths were set into church floors in North Africa, Italy, and France.

At the new millennium, we are in the midst of a great labyrinth renaissance. Caerdroia (a Welsh word meaning "Troy Town," an ancient word for labyrinths) was founded in Britain in 1980 to further the study of labyrinths. An exhibit in Milan in 1981 on labyrinths as archetypal images helped move labyrinths back into public consciousness, and individuals such as Sig Lonegren, author of *Labyrinths: Ancient Myths and Modern Uses*, helped continue the momentum. The Reverend Dr. Lauren Artress "rediscovered" the Chartres labyrinth during a workshop she attended in 1991 and has spearheaded the international movement to promote use of that labyrinth.

LABYRINTH THEMES

The labyrinth, echoing the spiral's transformational theme, has invited journeyers and spiritual seekers through the ages to contemplate the mysteries of life. From my study of labyrinth history, four themes in the symbolism and use of the labyrinth have emerged: death and rebirth; initiation, or symbolic death and rebirth; fertility; and the spiritual journey.

These same themes are important to today's walkers. Understanding them gives us a better sense of how to use the labyrinth in our own times for spiritual and transformational work.

DEATH AND REBIRTH

Labyrinths have been connected with funerary rites for thousands of years. These ancient funerals were different from ours, not only grieving the passing of the deceased but preparing their spirit for rebirth as well. The labyrinth's winding journey to center and back out again served as a map for this transition from life to death to rebirth.

The tomb in Sardinia is only one such example. Burial sites with stone labyrinths have also been found all along the Scandinavian coast, dating back to the Iron Age. Historians speculate that in the Chartres Cathedral labyrinth in France, choral dances may have been performed, and symbolic games played, that celebrated Christ's death and resurrection at Easter.

INITIATION

Cretan coins from A.D. 500 show many variants of the seven-circuit classical labyrinth (now sometimes called the Cretan labyrinth). The designs are thought to refer to the legendary labyrinth at Knossos, where Theseus killed the Minotaur imprisoned at the center.

This powerful myth has captured the imagination of storytellers and artists for centuries. A classic heroic initiation—in which a hero faces mortal challenges and emerges victorious—the myth has been retold as a story about the journey we must all make into our own shadows, in order to move back out into the world as fuller human beings.

Petroglyphs at Val Camonica in northern Italy dating from 1500 B.C., represent several labyrinths. The first has a haunting face composed of only staring eyes in the center. The second petroglyph shows an initiate fighting this face representing initiation, or death and rebirth, at the center of the labyrinth. Petroglyphs from southern India, dating as far back as 1000 B.C., tell the story of death, rebirth, and initiation, with warriors fighting around the labyrinth and being sacrificed in its center.

FERTILITY

As labyrinths were used to signify literal and symbolic death, so they were used to symbolize and celebrate birth and fertility. This celebration of new life, of fertility, stemmed from ancient myths, similar to the Greek myth of Demeter and Persephone, in which a goddess was temporarily released from the underworld to bring spring and fertility to the earth.

Ceremonies, fertility rites, and games, often tied in to seasonal events such as solstices and equinoxes, were celebrated in Scandinavian stone labyrinths. These events celebrated the return of sun, warmth, and fertility to a frozen earth, metaphorically symbolizing the resurgence of new life we all experience after challenging times. One popular game placed a maiden in the center of the labyrinth, with youths racing, or dancing in to "win" her. In fact, some labyrinths in Finland were known as virgin dances.

These seasonal fertility ceremonies and games, it is conjectured, were also carried out in the turf mazes of Europe. As late as the eighteenth century, young men in England would challenge one another to a race through the maze to win the young woman at the center.

THE SPIRITUAL JOURNEY

After the Crusades, when the pilgrimage to Jerusalem became more difficult and too dangerous, Christian pilgrims could journey to designated cathedrals and walk the labyrinth there as the final metaphorical stage of their pilgrimage to the holy city. The labyrinths were often known as the Road to Jerusalem, and the center of the labyrinth was called Jerusalem. In a bigger sense, the labyrinth walk was understood as being analogous to the earthly journey through life to heaven; the center was often called *ciel*, the French word for heaven.

The Pima culture of the American Southwest weaves the labyrinth, known as Siuku Ki, into their baskets. The design symbolizes for them the pathway leading to the top of Baboquiviri, their sacred mountain and the Sacred Center of their tribal lands. Likewise, for the Hopi, the circular labyrinth, known to them as the Mother Earth symbol, called Tapu'at (Mother and Child)—found carved in rocks near Hopi villages in Arizona and also carved on ceremonial sticks—represents the universal plan of the Creator to be followed as the Road of Life.

SACRED SPACE

Throughout time, labyrinths have represented sacred journey. Part of the power of this sacred journey stems from the power of the labyrinth as sacred space.

"Sacred space": What comes to mind? A church, synagogue, or mosque? An ancient sacred site, such as Stonehenge in southeastern England or a long-abandoned Anasazi kiva on a southwestern mesa? A shady spot beside your favorite stream or a mountaintop whose profound silence is broken only by the wind?

All of these are sacred spaces. In ancient Greek *temenos*, or "sacred precinct," originally signified sacred groves or wells; only later did the word come to mean temples. Sacred spaces, *temenae*, whether mountain or labyrinth or temple, invite us to right relation with Spirit. These places are, as mythologist and scholar Joseph Campbell once said, "a microcosm of the macrocosm," places where people can come to acknowledge and focus on who they really are, and in what, or whom, they place their ultimate trust.

The common elements of sacred space form the physical and energetic foundation for the labyrinth. You can walk the labyrinth without knowing anything about sacred space and still be transformed by the experience; it happened for me for many years that way. What I found, though, is that the experience of walking the labyrinth is immeasurably deepened by understanding the elements of sacred space. By being aware of how these elements are part of the labyrinth's power, you can work with them consciously as you walk.

"A sacred place is a certain physical location which contains us by giving us a place to be safe, nurtured, and supported in our totality—body, emotions, mind, and spirit," writes art therapist Roberta Beale, who works with the labyrinth as *temenos*, in *Dialogues with the Living Earth*. "Here we can explore anything and everything, into our deepest being and out into our farthest imaginings. . . . Being in a sacred place allows us to become resonant, again and again, with all that we . . . know to be sacred, and with all that we hold in the sacred spaces within us."

SACRED CIRCLES AND CENTERS

The circle has always symbolized wholeness, God, the cosmos. Sacred structures are often circular: basilicas, medicine wheels, stupas, labyrinths.

"Everything an Indian does is in a circle, and that is because the power of the world always works in circles, and everything tries to be round," says Native American shaman Black Elk. Throughout human history we have sat in circles, danced in circles, drawn circles on everything from cave walls to contemporary canvases. Remember the pictures of suns—circles of light and Self—you made as a child. Know that whenever you step foot in the labyrinth, you are within that sacred circle.

"God makes himself known to the world; He fills up the whole circle of the universe, but makes his particular abode in the center," wrote Christian theologian Lucian almost eighteen centuries ago. All circles, no matter how big or small, have centers, that place from which the circle itself is birthed.

Reaching center in the labyrinth is about reaching a focus of spiritual power and grace, the still point in the center of a chaotic world. After the twists and turns of the labyrinth's circuits, this still point mirrors the calm center of gravity deep in our own soul unaffected by the movement of our lives.

Cultures throughout time have depicted sacred circles and centers as mandalas. A mandala, the Sanskrit world for "circle," is a graphic representation of both cosmos and psyche, a circular diagram enclosing a divine center, a sacred state of consciousness. Mandalas function as maps inviting the viewer to remember the journey into wholeness and unity with the Sacred. Meditators traditionally enter the mandala in their imagination, working their way from perimeter to center, imaginal movement that mirrors the physical movement of walking the labyrinth.

Tibetans create elaborate mandalas on scrolls for meditators to reflect upon, evoking spiritual transformation; the sacred center of their world, Mount Meru, is itself a mandala. Navajo medicine men create sand mandalas to bring a sick person back in balance with spirit, thereby effecting healing. In workshops and therapy studios across the country today, people are drawing mandalas for emotional healing and spiritual growth.

To walk the labyrinth as a mandala is to embody that journey to our own sacred centers in a way that involves all of our being, body, soul, and spirit. The first time I ever made the connection between mandalas and labyrinths was during a workshop I led where participants drew mandalas as a meditation on wholeness and the spiritual journey. Later we walked the labyrinth. A participant told me that evening about her experience of walking the labyrinth as entering a mandala.

"It was as if I had walked into my own mandala," she recalled as we ate dinner. "The circle of the labyrinth became the perimeter of my drawing. With each step I moved closer to the center of my mandala. When I reached the center of the labyrinth it seemed, in my own body, like I had stepped into the center of my own drawing. I *became* the center of my drawing [a tree]. I spread my arms and became that tree and all it meant for me. My body got it, not just my mind like when I drew the mandala. I walked out with that tree growing in every cell of my body."

SACRED GEOMETRY

ircles, centers, spirals: All embody an ancient discipline called sacred geometry, from which derives a great deal of the labyrinth's proportion and power. In ancient times "geometry" meant the contemplation of forms, "a way by which the essential creative mystery is rendered visible," writes Robert Lawlor in *Sacred Geometry*. "The passage from the unmanifest, pure, formal ideas to the 'here-below,' the world that spins out from that original divine stroke, can be mapped out by geometry." Two important components of sacred geometry have a direct bearing upon the labyrinth: transcendental numbers and the Golden Mean.

Transcendental numbers—such as pi (the ratio of the circumference to the diameter of a circle, or 3.1415 . . .) and the square roots of two, three, and five—form the basis not only of sacred geometry but of sacred space and architecture throughout the world, including the labyrinth. The Golden Mean, called by many mathematicians the most essential pattern of wholeness found in creation, is an expression of relationship: a pattern whereby a smaller part of the pattern is in the same relationship to a larger part of the pattern as the larger part is to the whole. The Golden Mean and transcendental numbers determine the structure for all sacred architecture, from the Great Pyramid of Egypt to the Greek Parthenon to Borobudur, the world's largest Buddhist stupa, to the great Gothic cathedrals of Europe.

The Golden Mean also is the matrix for organic spirals in nature, determining the distribution of seeds in a sunflower, the proportions in the spiraling of a snail shell, the growth of a ram's horn, and the uncurling of fetuses in humans and animals. It represents both the magnificent unfolding of life itself and the invisible Sacred Pattern guiding this transformative process. This Golden Mean, invisibly

ROBERT FERRÉ

A canvas Chartres labyrinth by Robert Ferré.

spiraling in the labyrinth, invites us—even if we don't consciously know it—to participate in the unfolding of the world every time we walk its curves, birthing creation itself as we spiral to the center.

Labyrinth maker Robert Ferré was so awestruck when he discovered sacred geometry's power in the labyrinth that he worked for weeks learning to draw a labyrinth with nothing but a pencil and a straightedge. After years of study and labyrinth construction, he is still amazed by the power of these unseen formulas. "The incredible thing about the labyrinth is that it will not let itself be known in quantifiable terms. It can be drawn and walked and appreciated, but literally not quantified or known," says Ferré. "I think the power of the labyrinth is that it takes us way back to a prescientific time when our minds didn't rule our bodies, spirits, and souls. The labyrinth speaks directly to the proportions that we are all actually even made of. The idea of sacred geometry was to discover the sacred building blocks of creation itself. There's something very elemental about the labyrinth that speaks to who we really are at our deepest level, a much deeper level than the shallow one of modern society.

"This isn't conscious for us now; most people walk the labyrinth and don't know anything about sacred geometry. They do know, though, that something *very* powerful is going on that they are deeply touched by but don't understand. They say 'I don't know what this is, but *wow!*' They don't have words for this sort of profound experience of sacred geometry in the labyrinth, because it's older than our terribly impoverished vocabulary and way of seeing the world, but they know it. They just know it."

Alex Champion, a former biochemist and present creator of earthwork labyrinths, likens the labyrinth to a huge tuning fork, vibrating with the energy of sacred geometry. When we walk the labyrinth, he says, we are "contained within, and subject to, its energy field. Since the labyrinth is based upon sacred geometry, it's very good and powerful energy. It's like the labyrinth is ringing, and your body starts ringing sympathetically once you walk.

"If there are stuck blocks of energy inside your own energy field as a result of painful experiences in life, the longer you work with the labyrinth, the greater the chance that those blocks will get shaken loose, and shaken free, from all this vibrating. It's an incredible way to get garbage out of the body."

In our utilitarian culture we have lost all sense of the power of symbols and sacred space. Walking the labyrinth returns us to a pre–Scientific Revolution way of directly participating in the power of creation. Each time we spiral into the labyrinth we walk into a world that contains far more mystery and magic than our literal minds could ever grasp.

Part Two

Making the Labyrinth

CHAPTER FOUR

Making
Your Own Labyrinth

Imagine having your own labyrinth: Instead of having to drive twenty minutes to walk the labyrinth nearest you (if you are fortunate enough to have one nearby), you simply step out your back door or reach for a small finger labyrinth tucked away in a desk drawer or resting on a tabletop. Your own labyrinth can be walked day or night, on a whim, whenever the inspiration or the desire seizes you. You can walk in delicious solitude, or if you have a walking labyrinth you can have a great gathering and celebration, all on your own time.

If you have easy access to a labyrinth near you, that's great. Even better, though, is to have a labyrinth at your home—one to walk with either legs or fingers—or know how to construct a temporary one at a park or beach.

There are two good reasons to learn to make a labyrinth, from the simplest one drawn on paper to a more complex one in your backyard. First, if you take the time to learn how a labyrinth is constructed, your understanding of it will be broadened and deepened.

Sig Lonegren, author of *Labyrinths: Ancient Myths and Modern Uses*, differentiates between "knowing" about a labyrinth using your five senses and "gnowing" (derived from *gnosis*, the intuitive apprehension of a spiritual truth) a labyrinth using your intuitive, nonrational faculties. Once you "gnow" a labyrinth by drawing one and understanding how it is constructed from the inside out, you can carry its transformative pattern within you wherever you go.

Second, if you have your own labyrinth—even a paper one tucked in your desk drawer—you can use it whenever you wish. And if you don't have easy access to a labyrinth, constructing your own will be your only way to use this powerful tool.

Even if you have no interest at all in creating a labyrinth of either type, I still encourage you to read these chapters. You may change your mind once you see how powerful and creative a process it can be. Having easy access to a labyrinth will greatly enhance your explorations.

Even if you do nothing else, learn how to draw a labyrinth from the seed pattern. As Lonegren says, "gnowing" a labyrinth is an entirely different experience than "knowing" it. Even just learning how to draw a labyrinth—a very simple process—will enhance any work you do with the labyrinth.

Instructions are first given for drawing and creating a seven-circuit Cretan labyrinth. After you get the hang of this one, instructions are given for creating a modified Chartres labyrinth.

To begin, you will draw a seven-circuit labyrinth from a simple seed pattern. After you get to "gnow" a labyrinth in this way, instructions will be given for making several different kinds of finger labyrinths, portable ones you can "walk" with fingers rather than feet. Even if you have neither desire nor space to build a larger labyrinth, make a finger labyrinth. If you plan to build a walking labyrinth, making a finger one is a great dress rehearsal, enabling you to build a larger one with more ease and confidence.

PRACTICING THE SEED PATTERN

*L*earn to draw a labyrinth to get the "feel" for how one is made. The more you understand the basic construction by drawing it, the easier it will be for you to lay out your labyrinth, whether finger or larger. If the word "draw" sets off alarms, please understand that drawing a labyrinth requires absolutely no artistic ability. Drawing a labyrinth from a seed pattern is simply a matter of connecting the dots.

The seed pattern or matrix of the classical labyrinth is shown in Figure 4.1A. The seed pattern is an equal armed cross, bordered by four right angles and a dot in each corner. Once you have assembled these elements—cross, right angles, and dots—you can easily draw a seven-circuit classical labyrinth.

To draw the seed pattern for the seven-circuit labyrinth, you'll need graph paper with $\frac{1}{4}$-inch or $\frac{1}{2}$-inch squares and a pencil. Follow the step-by-step instructions in Figure 4.1, moving from A to I, to "gnow" a seven-circuit labyrinth. Photocopy the instructions before beginning. Make several copies so that if you feel confused, you can draw over the relevant diagram.

When you have assembled your materials, find a place where you can be undisturbed for half an hour. Put on some music if you'd like. Acknowledge that you're at the beginning of the adventure of getting to "gnow" a labyrinth. No matter how much you've walked the labyrinth before, this process will deepen your experience of walking it. Before you begin drawing, read through the following steps several times and examine the diagrams.

1. Beginning several squares lower than the center of your graph paper, make a cross four squares, or units, high and four units wide. Draw four right angles, each leg one unit long, at the corners of the cross. Now place four dots one unit away from the four right angles; starting with the dot at the lower-left-hand corner and moving clockwise, label

FIGURE 4.1: HOW TO DRAW AND "GNOW" A LABYRINTH

FIGURE 4.1A

FIGURE 4.1B

FIGURE 4.1C

FIGURE 4.1D

FIGURE 4.1E

FIGURE 4.1F

FIGURE 4.1G

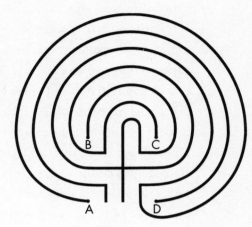

FIGURE 4.1H

FIGURE 4.1I

the dots A, B, C, and D. The corresponding right angles will also be referred to as angles A, B, C and D. Draw this seed pattern on sheets of paper until you "gnow" it; it will form the basis for your labyrinth drawings and later labyrinth construction if you so choose.

2. Draw an arc from the top arm of the cross on your graph paper to the top leg of angle C. This arcing up and over from one element (cross arm, angle leg, or dot) on the left-hand side of the page to a *different* element on the right-hand side is the basic movement for drawing the entire labyrinth.

3. Draw an arc from the top leg of angle B to dot C. If you start feeling confused (as I did during my first attempts), take a deep breath and keep going. This spatial confusion is often part of the learning curve. You will move through it and understand the labyrinth better than you ever could have by simply looking at an illustration.

4. Arc a line from the next available spot on the left, which is dot B, to the next available place on the right, which is the lower leg of angle C.

5. The next open spot on the left is the lower leg of angle B; make an arc from it to the right arm of the central cross.

6. Continue arcing lines from the next available element (arm, leg, or dot) on the left-hand side to the next available element on the right-hand side (which, remember, will always be a different element).

7. The final arc will connect the lower leg of angle A to the bottom arm of the central cross. When you have connected these, you also have created the entrance to the labyrinth.

Congratulations! You've created what is called a left-handed labyrinth (so named because the first turn in walking this model is to the left). For simplicity's sake, we'll be working with this type of labyrinth. If you wish to create a right-handed labyrinth, simply reverse all of the preceding instructions, arcing from right to left. Mirror the

Wooden finger labyrinths by Neal Harris.

entire illustration. By so doing you will create a labyrinth whose first turn is to the right.

Draw this left-handed labyrinth at least ten times, as Lonegren suggests, but not at one sitting! This will allow you to construct any labyrinth, small or large, from a place of deeper confidence and understanding.

FINGER LABYRINTHS

*F*inger labyrinths are small labyrinths meant to be "walked" with a finger tracing the circuits, preferably a finger from your non-dominant hand. "Walking" a finger labyrinth produces the same physiological, emotional, and spiritual effects as a larger labyrinth. You can stop at the entrance to a finger labyrinth and pray or close your eyes and meditate at the center, just as you can with a larger labyrinth. You also can use the finger labyrinth for healing work, goal setting, fostering creativity, or any of the other uses for the labyrinth you will learn about later in this book. You may use a finger labyrinth just as easily as a larger walking one for any exercise.

Finger labyrinths, which can be made or purchased in a variety of materials, are eminently portable. You can even keep a laminated paper labyrinth in your desk at work, ready to be unobtrusively "walked" after a stressful meeting or phone call, or to help get your creative juices flowing for a project. I keep a beautiful purple heart-wood labyrinth on a table altar by the entrance to my therapy studio. Clients sometimes walk it while waiting for a session. I like to use my finger labyrinth when I don't have the time for a "regular" walk. In fact, spending even a couple of minutes with my finger labyrinth allows me to become centered.

Unlike outdoor labyrinths, you can use a finger labyrinth any time of the day or night or in any weather. I have "walked" my wooden labyrinth many times in the stillness of the predawn darkness. When I am too caught up in a problem or too engrossed in a creative project to sleep, I take my finger labyrinth and a candle to the sofa. After lighting the candle and asking for guidance, I "walk" the finger labyrinth just as I'd walk the larger outside one. After I finish the walk, I meditate or journal on what I learned. Having a finger labyrinth in your home also allows for "walking" when it is snowing, sweltering, or pelting freezing rain outside.

I find that keeping my finger labyrinth visible and "walkable" in my home changes the tenor of my day, even if I don't use it for several weeks. I walk by my finger labyrinth whenever I make the transition from "householder" in my house to writer or therapist in my studio connected to the kitchen. The labyrinth reminds me that all the aspects of my life—mother, partner, teacher, therapist, writer—are sacred journeys, if I can remember to honor their varied paths. When I find myself caught up in worrying or trying too hard, simply tracing a circuit or two, or touching center, brings me back to my own center.

Beautiful wooden finger labyrinths, both seven and eleven circuit, can be purchased. You can make photocopies of labyrinth drawings or order paper labyrinths and paint the paper, then cover with clear paper for durability. These paper labyrinths can be stashed in desk drawers or tucked in briefcases for traveling. (See the appendix for sources.)

You also can create your own finger labyrinth and decorate it any way you'd like, making it truly your own.

MAKING A FINGER LABYRINTH

Before you make a walking labyrinth, I recommend that you make a finger labyrinth, either a simple paper one or a three-dimensional one. A paper labyrinth is the simplest to create. You can draw your own, order a paper labyrinth, or photocopy and enlarge one of the diagrams in this book.

Although you can walk an unadorned paper labyrinth, I suggest decorating the paper to individualize it and make it your own. Use crayons, colored pencils, or watercolors. Allow at least a half an hour of uninterrupted time. If you wish, put some quiet music on. Gather your materials at a table. Put your labyrinth drawing in front of you and trace its circuits from entrance to center, and back out again, with one finger from your nondominant hand.

Now place the palm of your nondominant hand on the center of the labyrinth and close your eyes. Take some deep slow breaths. Feel your inbreath filling your heart, opening and softening it. Feel your outbreath flowing from your heart down through the arm of your nondominant hand and out your palm into the center of the labyrinth. You also can imagine your outbreath as a current of light flowing into the center of the labyrinth. See, or feel, the labyrinth filling with light, chi, Spirit.

As you breathe into the labyrinth, ask for images that connect you more deeply with it. You may become aware of a particular color or colors. You might see an image in the center of the labyrinth, something concrete such as a flower or abstract like a spiral. Continue breathing into the labyrinth until it feels "full" or until you feel done.

Open your eyes and draw or paint your labyrinth with anything you have seen. It's important to remember that this isn't an art contest; your drawing or painting is for you, and no one else. Draw or paint until your labyrinth feels finished.

When it is dry, cover the front and back of the paper with clear self-adhesive paper. This simple labyrinth can go with you to your office and stay in a drawer to be pulled out for destressing, problem solving, or creativity enhancement, all of which you will learn in the following chapters. It also travels beautifully in a briefcase.

You also can laminate just the front, and attach the paper to a piece of cardboard or foam board with rubber cement for a stiffer and more durable "walking" surface.

Your second option for a finger labyrinth is to construct one from foam board, canvas panel (found in art supply stores), or plywood, and rope or clothesline. Although slightly less portable, this labyrinth allows for more meditative "walking": Since the walls of the paths will be raised, you won't have to watch to stay on the paths, freeing your mind and spirit.

These instructions will help you create a classical seven-circuit labyrinth measuring approximately 14 by 16 inches. You can make your labyrinth smaller or larger by changing the size of the basic unit, which is one inch.

To make this labyrinth you'll need:

- Canvas panel or foam board, available at art supply and craft shops, that measures at least 17 by 17 inches or a piece of plywood cut to the same dimensions
- Eighteen feet of thin cotton rope such as clothesline for the walls of the circuits, or small stones or shells
- Good glue, such as E-6000, available in arts and crafts or hardware stores
- Ruler and pencil
- Materials to decorate your labyrinth (choose whatever media attract you most): paints, pictures cut from magazines, glitter, crayons

Lay out your supplies, put some favorite music on if you wish, and refer back to Figure 4.1.

1. Begin by drawing lines, both vertical and horizontal, one inch apart across a 17-inch by 17-inch area in the center of the board, so that you end up with a grid of one-inch squares, or units. If you wish to make your finger labyrinth larger or smaller, simply adjust the area of the squares; for instance, by making your unit two-inches square rather than one-inch square, you'll have a 34-inch labyrinth rather than a 17-inch labyrinth.

2. Refer to Figure 4.1H. Notice that the center of the labyrinth is not in the exact geometrical center. Due to the way the labyrinth is constructed, its top "half" is larger than its bottom "half." The center of the labyrinth you're making, where you'll draw the seed pattern, is not in the center of the grid you have drawn. To find the starting place for your seed pattern, mark off an area 15 units across by 14 vertical units. Count down 10 units from the top, 7 units from the left side, and 8 units from the right. This is the starting point for your seed pattern.

3. Draw an equal-armed cross here (two units for each arm), and add the right angles and dots as you did when you drew the seed pattern. Draw the labyrinth as you did on paper.

4. When you have drawn the labyrinth, find Figure 4.2. Secure the end of the rope at point B with glue. Lay down a line of glue and place the rope on the glue until you come to the end of that line at point D. Cut the rope, and put a little glue on the end to prevent fraying.

5. Lay down the next length of rope beginning at point A, continuing until you intersect at point E with the previously laid down rope. Cut the rope so that the end lies flush at a right angle against the previously laid down rope, then pick up again with a new piece right on the other side of the same rope at point F. Continue with this rope until you reach the end at point C.

   If you make your walls from beads or shells, simply place

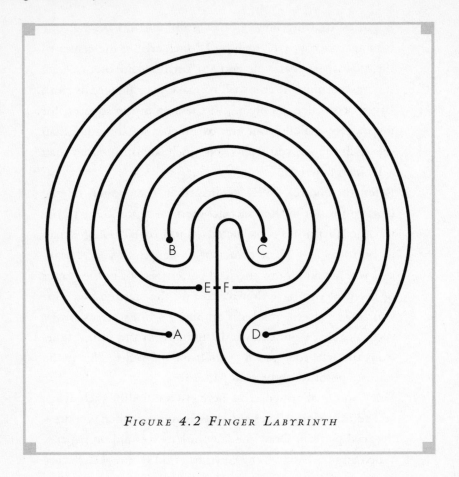

FIGURE 4.2 FINGER LABYRINTH

them along the lines, making sure they fit well before gluing.

6. You've done it! Let the glue dry. Repeat the meditation from the beginning of this section on making finger labyrinths, using the labyrinth you've just made instead of a paper labyrinth, and then decorate the labyrinth any way you'd like.

Before you "walk" it for the first time, read the section in Chapter 5 on dedicating a labyrinth. It's fun to dedicate finger labyrinths as well as larger ones, and I believe doing so draws in additional energy and power for you to work with on subsequent "walks."

Remember, as you read the rest of the book, that you can use your finger labyrinth for any of the ways suggested for walking, and working with, the labyrinth. Even if you decide to make your own large labyrinth, you can return, as I do, to your finger labyrinth for the same purposes as the larger labyrinth, when you are constrained by weather, time of day, or amount of time available.

Now that you "gnow" the labyrinth, you may find that the idea of your own larger labyrinth—either as a permanent part of your house or garden or as part of time spent outdoors at a park or on a hike—seems more possible, and more intriguing. Even if you don't have immediate plans to build a larger labyrinth, I encourage you to read the next two chapters.

CHAPTER FIVE

Creating a Walking Labyrinth

J don't know how to build a labyrinth. How could I possibly do *that*?" People who have never built a labyrinth often ask Jean Lutz this question, hands thrown up in helplessness.

"Making a labyrinth isn't magic," replies Lutz, editor of *The Labyrinth Letter*. "It's a lot easier than you think. Just *do* it."

Give yourself permission to have "beginner's mind," creating a labyrinth in the spirit of adventure and love. Allow plenty of leeway to experiment, make mistakes, and enjoy and learn from the process of building a labyrinth. As Lutz emphasizes, what is most important is not technical perfection but your desire to make a labyrinth and the quality of attention and consciousness you bring to the process itself.

Gretchen Schodde, who has built three labyrinths at Harmony Hill and helped construct many others, compares building a labyrinth for the first time to trying a new exotic recipe made with unfamiliar ingredients. "When you try a new recipe," says Schodde, "you prepare yourself to make something unfamiliar that will not only feed the body but nourish the soul. This is just like preparing to make a labyrinth for the first time. First you study the recipe. When you're done with that step you gather the ingredients. Then, when you're ready to go—whether in cooking or labyrinth making—you allow yourself to be as relaxed and focused as possible. The attitude with which you approach making the labyrinth, just like cooking, affects, in so many intangible but powerful ways, the final product, whether it's a new dish or a new labyrinth."

There are six steps involved in the process of making a labyrinth:

1. Clarifying your intention
2. Choosing the type of labyrinth and materials
3. Siting the labyrinth
4. Consecrating the space and the construction process
5. Constructing the labyrinth
6. Dedicating the labyrinth

Read through each section first. Notice that step 5, Constructing the Labyrinth, is not included in this chapter, but is the entirety of Chapter 6. Read that chapter as well, referring to its diagrams.

Before you start, allow me to let you in on a little secret: *If I can make a labyrinth, so can you.* Spatial orientation is not my forte, to put it mildly. I get lost driving to the drugstore. After I moved into my new home, it took me several months to choose which of the two traffic arteries, each within three blocks of my house, I should take and have some confidence that I'd actually end up on the right street in the right direction. No kidding.

So, if I can make a labyrinth, so can you. If you've taken the time to "gnow" the labyrinth through drawing it, can follow a recipe, and can give yourself and anyone who helps you permission to relax and enjoy the process, you will soon have yourself a new labyrinth for exploration, learning, and healing.

ROBERT FERRÉ

A seven-circuit labyrinth made of gravel and grass in St. Louis, Missouri.

CLARIFY YOUR REASONS
FOR MAKING A LABYRINTH

Jean Lutz claims that your reasons for building a labyrinth are the most important ingredients when constructing a labyrinth. "Nothing else—layout, materials, preparation—is as important as your purpose for building the labyrinth," says Lutz. "With a clear intention you can build a tiny three-circuit labyrinth in a court-yard, and it would be a powerful labyrinth. It doesn't make any difference, all the rest of it: the foundation of the labyrinth is your intent."

Ask yourself and have all others involved in the process of building the labyrinth ask themselves as well:

- Why do I want to build a labyrinth?
- What do I hope to get from actually making a labyrinth?
- Why is it important to me that I have my own labyrinth?

TOBY EVANS

An aerial view of the Prairie Labyrinth in Sibley, Missouri. The Prairie Labyrinth is a seven-circuit labyrinth with four-foot wide paths mown into native prairie grasses.

- What do I hope to get from walking and working with this labyrinth once it has been created?

Labyrinths are being built all over the country for many reasons: They are being created specifically for healing from cancer and other diseases, for working with learning disabilities, for bringing in the millennium, for individual meditation. Your reasons can range from one or more specific purposes to a more general intention. Some possibilities include:

- The need to eliminate stress in your life
- A way of meditation that involves your body as well as your soul
- Becoming more attuned to the land and the cycles of seasons
- Fostering community
- Healing from a specific illness or disease
- Celebrating the deeper meaning of holidays such as New Year's or a solstice or equinox

ROBERT FERRÉ

Building a turf labyrinth in Michigan.

- Celebrating or ritualizing an important event, such as a birthday, an adolescent coming of age, or the blessing of a new home

PERMANENT OR TEMPORARY: SELECTING THE MATERIALS

PERMANENT LABYRINTHS

*Y*ou can construct a permanent labyrinth in your backyard, family room, or basement. You also can make one on the grounds of a church, school, hospital, or community center, or in a meeting room or auditorium. A permanent labyrinth will always be there for the walking, with no time spent setting it up after the original construction.

The two primary challenges of a permanent labyrinth are the amount of space required (a 25-foot-square minimum for comfortable walking) and the upkeep. Labyrinth maintenance is a soothing meditative practice

ROBERT FERRÉ

A Chartres labyrinth made from stone and mulch in St. Louis, Missouri.

in itself, but it does require a certain investment of time depending on the materials used, from labor-intensive garden labyrinths to painted concrete labyrinths that just require broom sweeping.

While stones are most commonly used to mark outdoor pathways, other outdoor options to mark the walls of the circuits include:

- Rope, plants, shells, bricks, or pavers
- Mown grass as the path, unmown grass for the walls
- Mown grass as the path, with slim walls dug out and filled to grass level with bricks or sand
- Turf labyrinths: a dug-out path below ground level that is filled with sand or bark chips (if you decide to use bark chips or mulch, look for the sliver-free kind that is used in playgrounds); walls of circuits can be reinforced with brick or stone and tops of walls planted with flowers or low shrubbery
- Mound labyrinths: similar to turf labyrinths, except that instead of the paths being dug out to below ground level, the walls are berms, raised mounds of earth. Again, the tops of the walls may be planted

ANNETTE REYNOLDS

- Paint on a concrete driveway or patio
- Paint, stain, tiles, or even inlaid wood for indoor permanent labyrinths

TEMPORARY LABYRINTHS

There are two types of temporary labyrinths: constructed ones that can be dismantled easily and portable ones painted on a variety of fabrics, which can be laid down for walking and stored until the next use.

Temporarily constructed labyrinths can be made indoors or out: in your yard, in parks, at the beach, or on any kind of floor, if the dimensions of the room are at least 25 feet square. They require no maintenance, since they are dismantled after use. They can't, however, be used spontaneously, since even the simplest temporary labyrinth requires at least an hour of setup time. Walking a temporary labyrinth at a beach or park can open one's eyes in new ways to the beauty of place.

Outdoor temporary labyrinths can be made from:

ANNETTE REYNOLDS

- Rope or ribbon staked to the ground or stapled to sticks
- Lime
- Cornmeal
- Feathers (Marty Cain, a professional labyrinth builder in Vermont, once created a temporary labyrinth entirely from thousands of white turkey feathers!)
- Football turf paint
- Snow or sand

Indoor temporary labyrinths can be made from:

- Masking or electrical tape
- Rope, yarn, or ribbon taped to the floor at intervals
- Cornmeal

Portable labyrinths are "temporary" only in the sense that they are laid down for specific occasions, then taken up and stored until the next use. They can be painted on canvas, sheets, or ripstop nylon, or laminated vinyl-on-vinyl. They are more or less conveniently portable, depending on the weight of material used. They are also more or less

ANNETTE REYNOLDS

durable, ranging from the high durability of canvas to the fragility of sheets. Several suppliers sell portable labyrinths in different stages of completion for different prices; please see the appendix for information. You also can, if you are enterprising and patient, draw and paint your own portable fabric labyrinth.

SITING YOUR LABYRINTH

If you're building an outside labyrinth, go sit in the area you've chosen. Get quiet and ask for guidance for where the labyrinth should be, including the placement of the entrance. If the labyrinth needs to be in a particular place due to space limitations or garden layout, ask permission for it to be there. "Asking permission is a form of politeness in the metaphysical realm," says Alex Champion, former biophysicist and professional labyrinth and maze maker. "Contact the local spirits and ask permission for building the labyrinth. Ask for help to determine the orientation of the labyrinth and the best place for its entrance. If you haven't done this sort of thing before, just use your intuition. Go out there and find a site that just feels right to you. When you ask for permission, do you feel resistance in

NEAL HARRIS

A canvas seven-circuit labyrinth created by Neal and Mary Harris.

the form of heaviness or fogginess? A 'yes' will leave you feeling light and clear."

Don't just ask the spirits of the land. Ask the to-be-made labyrinth, as well. "After you have determined where the labyrinth is to be built," suggests Neal Harris, builder of the Earth Wisdom Labyrinth, "ask the labyrinth which direction it wants to open to, so that it's in harmony with nature and the land. I feel it's extremely important to tune in to where the labyrinth itself wants to be situated. Labyrinths know where they want—and need—to be."

Other makers suggest lining up the quarters of the labyrinth with the compass points of the four directions, the entrance to the labyrinth facing east. Mary Ellen Johnson and the volunteer building crew at Unity Church of Bellevue decided to orient the labyrinth so that when a walker entered the labyrinth he or she would be facing the exact place where the sun rose on Summer Solstice. "We called Jeff Renner, our local weatherman," says Johnson, "and asked him for the coordinates of Summer Solstice sunrise. Then we found a surveyor who located those coordinates on the land we had set aside for the labyrinth."

ROBERT FERRÉ

Walking Robert Ferré's canvas seven-circuit labyrinth at St. Luke's Hospital, St. Louis, Missouri.

If you're creating an indoor labyrinth, take time to sit quietly in the middle of the room you've chosen. Orient yourself to the space. Imagine the earth underneath the building, no matter how far off the ground the room is situated. Ask permission of the earth beneath you to build a labyrinth.

No matter where and what kind of labyrinth you build, once you've made the decision to create a labyrinth, begin to relate to it as a real being, even though it is not yet "birthed." "After experiencing the incredible way the Earth Wisdom Labyrinth was pushing me before it was even built, it became so obvious to me that these labyrinths have a life of their own," recalls Neal Harris. "The labyrinth wouldn't let me alone during the time it took to build it. When I tried to meditate, questions kept coming up: Do you want to use this type of rock, or that type? The labyrinth definitely wanted to be birthed. I wasn't a reluctant birth mother, but I was definitely a hardworking birth mother!"

After moving into a new home, I dreamed one night about a labyrinth on the lawn sloping down to Thornton Creek. In the dream

The Peace Labyrinth at Unity Church of Bellevue, Washington.

I watched the labyrinth's circuits, made of liquid light, flowing to the center like water. I woke up knowing that I had been given marching orders by Spirit to build a labyrinth, not just for my family's personal and professional use but to bring light and coherence to a house and property that often surged with chaotic energies.

As I explored for several days what sort of labyrinth to build, I was astonished to feel the near-constant presence of this labyrinth beside and within me. Like Neal, I felt almost pregnant with the labyrinth-to-be. It was not some theoretical blueprint; it was a living, breathing reality, waiting to be birthed in my backyard.

If you feel stuck in any stage of the decision-making process, from clarifying the intention all the way through deciding how to consecrate it, try asking the labyrinth itself for input. You may find that it has definite ideas to share with you!

The author in a temporary rope labyrinth in Seattle, Washington.

CONSECRATING THE SPACE

Consecrate the space, and the construction process itself, before you begin building the labyrinth. You can do this in many ways, from a simple prayer to an elaborate ceremony.

Mary Ellen Johnson and her crew at Unity Church of Bellevue held a ground blessing ceremony before beginning construction. They sang favorite songs, after which they blessed the ground with water from the Jordan River. Johnson felt that the consecration was a very important part of the process. "After the consecration and during the construction, we all had a very strong sense that the earth was welcoming the construction. It felt to me and several others that all we were doing was uncovering the labyrinth, like it had been there all along."

When I decided to build a labyrinth, I sited it on the lawn behind our house. Before my friend Peter and I began laying down the rope, I sat in the center of the labyrinth-to-be and meditated. I called down light from the heavens and grounding stability up from the earth, visualizing the energies meeting and forming a vortex of light centered over the entire property. As this vortex tightened I watched it gather and integrate the irregular energies on the property that had so disturbed Peter and me. I witnessed in wonder the energy of the land and house flowing into, and becoming integrated with, this coherent pattern of light.

The vortex tightened after integrating the chaotic energies present and moved down into the space marked for the labyrinth. As it did so the light shifted from the spiral of the vortex into the circuits of the labyrinth, resembling the original dream image of currents of light flowing through the labyrinth into the center. Peter and I were planning another sort of consecration, but after this spontaneous meditation we realized that the blessing had already occurred.

Alex Champion says a small prayer he has developed over the years before breaking ground for construction of a new earth labyrinth. "We ask that God look upon this job with blessing and love. We ask that the people who work on this job do so without injury. We also ask that all the local spirits who are God's agents be here to support and advise us during the job. We ask especially that Mother Earth be present and bless the materials that are being used. We ask that the energy that comes in as this symbol is being made be of the highest and purest type and stay as long as at least 50 percent of this structure is still here. We ask that any energy present here now or in the future that isn't of the highest type be transformed and recycled by the spirits present. We ask that all experiences of all who use this labyrinth be for their highest good."

Take some time to think about how you'd like to articulate your intention for the labyrinth in the consecration. You also can include, as Champion does, a prayer for all the walkers-to-be and a thank-you to the spirits of that particular place for allowing you to build your labyrinth.

Spirit, I'm convinced, graciously acknowledges any consecration; what is important is that it is done. Gretchen Schodde and I wanted to make a seven-circuit labyrinth on the floor of a community build-ing at Harmony Hill before a cancer retreat so that participants could have a dry walk in our rainy Northwest winter. The labyrinth's con-struction, though, was delayed for over a month due to workmen insulating the building and installing a new heater under the floor.

We were finally left with just an hour one Saturday morning to create the labyrinth before I had to take a ferry back to Seattle. We worked as a team: Gretchen placed the first pieces of tape to mark the labyrinth as I said prayers at each of the four directions and the cen-ter of the labyrinth. I called upon the qualities represented by each of the four directions, and corresponding elements of earth, air, fire, and water, to be present in the labyrinth and bless all walkers with ground-edness, perspective and insight, passion and creativity, and healing. Gretchen added her prayers for each direction out loud as she worked. Finally I stood at the center and asked that the love and transformational energies of the Sacred move through and heal all who walked the labyrinth, particularly the ten participants coming later in the week for the retreat.

When I finished I thanked Spirit for understanding the slight ass-backwardness of consecrating the space while we were actually mak-ing the labyrinth. I got the impression of a large cosmic grin and a sense of approval that I was learning flexibility. The labyrinth emerged as a very powerful one, blessing the participants the following week and those who have since walked its circuits.

DEDICATING THE LABYRINTH

Dedicate the new labyrinth in a way that works best for you, but do it consciously. "Each group has to figure out what is impor-tant for them and the labyrinth," says Neal Harris. "You've got to have the ceremony, no matter how simple, be something that blesses the labyrinth and invites Mother Nature to commit her energies."

Alex Champion repeats a prayer as he first walks a new labyrinth by himself for its dedication. "Thank you for the opportunity to make this labyrinth, and we bless it in the name of All That Is. We surround this labyrinth with a bubble of divine white light filled with love and protection. May all who walk this labyrinth be balanced, centered, and grounded; have peace and happiness; be healed according to their needs; have their hearts filled with unconditional love. May the energy of this labyrinth always be pure and of the highest quality. If anyone walking this labyrinth releases nonbeneficial energy, we humbly ask the local spirits to transform and recycle it. May the experiences of all who walk this labyrinth be for their highest good."

As Champion walks, he sometimes holds his hands over the earthen walls and envisions his prayer suffusing them, so that the energy of the prayer will surround all who will ever walk the labyrinth.

When Neal Harris and his team finished constructing the massive Earth Wisdom Labyrinth, 150 people assembled for the dedication.

"We had a very powerful dedication ceremony," recalls Harris. Participants first smudged themselves with sage for purification while ringing bells and "drumming the heartbeat of Mother Earth." They then gathered in a circle around the labyrinth and honored and called into the labyrinth energies of the seven directions as well as those of the ancestors, the grandmothers and grandfathers. "We then brought in as a rainbow the energy of all the labyrinths from all over the world that have ever been, or are now. People visualized the energy of the labyrinths as rainbows coming from all directions, with one side of the rainbow in the center of the other labyrinth, arching into the center of our labyrinth that we were activating. To honor the process of giving and receiving, we sent back the healing energy of this labyrinth that was being activated to all the other labyrinths to increase their strength. It was so exciting to feel all that energy as people focused and brought it all in."

For your dedication, you can create a ceremony as rich as Harris's or as simple as walking the new labyrinth with an awareness of dedicating it.

CHAPTER SIX

Constructing Your Labyrinth

N ow you are ready to make a walking labyrinth. The first two sets of instructions are for a seven-circuit Cretan labyrinth; the last instructions are for an eleven-circuit Chartres labyrinth. Read through these instructions several times. If you have made a finger labyrinth, as you read the instructions for the larger labyrinth follow along with your finger.

The figures are key to understanding how to create a labyrinth. Constructing a labyrinth is primarily a visual and kinesthetic experience; the words are just to help move you along. If you don't understand a particular step, spend time with the corresponding figure. Read the instructions out loud, trace the step with your finger, and imagine actually constructing as you go. It also helps to have someone else to go over the instructions with you before you begin, to help make sure you understand them.

I suggest photocopying all the figures for the labyrinth you choose to make, so you can have them for easy reference during

ANNETTE REYNOLDS

ANNETTE REYNOLDS

construction. Then you also can make notes directly on the figures to help in the construction of future labyrinths.

The rope-and-tape Cretan labyrinths differ in one way from the finger and paper labyrinths you have been making. Turn now to Figure 6.1. Notice that the center is wider than the one you have been drawing. This wider center accommodates more people than the cen-

MELISSA REYNOLDS

ter of the traditional Cretan labyrinth. This form of the Cretan labyrinth also is easier to construct than one with a smaller center.

Instructions are given for three different ways to make the labyrinth:

- A temporary indoor Cretan labyrinth made from masking or electrical tape. You can adapt these instructions to create a permanent stone labyrinth outside.
- A rope Cretan labyrinth. Instructions are given for outside construction. Once you've made the labyrinth, you can dismantle the materials and store them in a duffel bag, to take with you to make a labyrinth wherever you'd like outdoors, space permitting.
- A temporary Chartres labyrinth made from masking tape.

Before you site the labyrinth, determine the amount of space you'll need. The paths can be anywhere from eighteen inches wide, the minimum for a comfortable walk, to as wide as you'd like. The width you choose can be based on function—Robert Ferré likes three-foot-wide paths in order to accommodate wheelchairs. Toby

ROBERT FERRÉ

A 104-foot masking tape labyrinth in St. Louis, Missouri.

Evans makes the mown-grass paths on her Prairie Labyrinth four feet wide since her rider mower cuts a four-foot swath.

A classical seven-circuit Cretan labyrinth is actually fifteen circuits wide by fourteen circuits deep; since you'll be creating labyrinths that have an extra-wide center, your labyrinths will be sixteen circuits wide rather than fifteen. That translates to a minimum of a square 25 feet by 25 feet if you use 18-inch-wide paths.

If you're building the labyrinth in a room, remember to allow at least one foot or so around the perimeter of the labyrinth so people aren't bumping against walls!

MAKING A CRETAN LABYRINTH WITH TAPE

This method of constructing a tape labyrinth with a larger center comes directly from Robert Ferré, labyrinth maker and director of the St. Louis Labyrinth Project, to whom I owe many thanks for these instructions. This method will create a seven-circuit labyrinth with an expanded center (see Figure 6.1), which will accommodate

FIGURE 6.1 CRETAN LABYRINTH WITH EXPANDED CENTER

more people in the center than the traditional seven-circuit labyrinth. For easy reference, photocopy all the figures used to construct the tape labyrinth. This way you can make notes on the copies to help you when constructing other labyrinths.

Materials

- One-inch-wide masking or electrical tape (approximately 450 feet for two-foot-wide paths). Buy extra tape, for a total of 500 feet. You can always return it, but it is better to have extra on hand than to have to run to the store.

FIGURE 6.2: FINISHED TAPE LABYRINTH

FIGURE 6.2A
Half circles with tape marks

FIGURE 6.2B
Filled in half circles

FIGURE 6.2C
Quarter circle tape
marks from B and C

FIGURE 6.2D
Filled in quarter circles

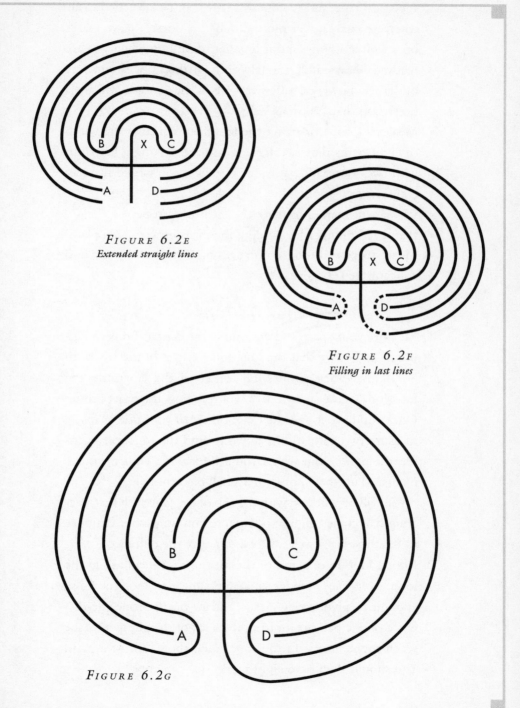

FIGURE 6.2E
Extended straight lines

FIGURE 6.2F
Filling in last lines

FIGURE 6.2G

Electrical tape, unlike adhesive tape, can be stretched easily to create curves; it is more durable; it doesn't leave marks on a wooden floor; and it is easier to pull up when you are ready to disassemble the labyrinth. If the floor is concrete or carpet, however, adhesive tape is stickier and will do a better job than electrical tape.

- Measuring rope or string the length of which is the width of eight paths plus two feet. If you are making a labyrinth with two-foot-wide paths, for instance, you would need an eighteen-foot rope.
- Permanent marker to mark the measuring rope.
- Plumber's plunger for holding the measuring rope in place.
- Music to play during construction to help you relax and concentrate (optional).

Instructions

1. Measure your space and determine the center. Look at Figure 6.2g. Notice that the functional center of the labyrinth is not the exact geometrical center of the labyrinth; the functional center is two path widths below the exact center. Once you have found the exact center of your usable space, measure two path widths down to find the functional center, the point from which you'll be making your measurements. Mark that spot with a small piece of tape.

   You will be working with the top of the labyrinth first, creating half circles. Figure out where you want your entrance to be; these half circles will be opposite the entrance.

2. Knot a loop in one end of the measuring rope and slip the loop over the plunger, making sure the loop is loose enough to pivot freely. Make a mark on the rope the distance of one path width from the stick of the plunger. Make seven more marks on the rope, each the width of a path. You should then have eight marks on your rope.

Secure the plunger over the center mark (X) with tape.

3. Refer to figure 6.2a for steps 3 to 5. Pull the rope so that it is straight, then lay it down at the bottom left of the half circles. Place a small piece of tape under each of the marks on the rope.

4. Pivot the rope a few degrees clockwise, and repeat step 3.

5. Keep pivoting the rope around the top half until you reach the other side. You now have eight concentric half circles of markers around your center point.

6. See Figure 6.2b. Take longer sections of tape and connect the dots, so to speak, creating lines. You now have created the top half of your labyrinth.

7. See Figure 6.2c. Move the plunger to point B and tape it down. Draw quarter circles from point B by placing tape under the first five marks on the rope. Notice that these five quarter circles connect with the five outer semicircles above them.

8. See Figure 6.2c. Move the plunger to point C and tape it down. Draw quarter circles from point C by placing tape under the first six marks on the rope. Notice that these six quarter circles connect with the six outer semicircles above them.

8. Connect all of the small pieces of tape with longer tape. Your labyrinth will now look like Figure 6.2d.

9. Refer to Figure 6.2e for steps 9 to 11. Move to the lower right quarter circles. Take the measuring rope off the plunger, and extend each of these five lines straight to the left by one rope mark. Place a piece of tape under the rope mark.

10. Connect the line nearest the center in the lower-left-hand quadrant with the line nearest the center in the lower-right-hand quadrant with a length of tape.

11. With tape, create a vertical line running from the unfinished

Creating a seven-circuit labyrinth from electrical tape.

line located to the left of the center dot down to the level of the outside circle on the left side.

12. See Figure 6.2f. To complete the labyrinth, create two half circles around points A and D and a quarter circle connecting the vertical line coming down from center with the outside line on the right side.

Congratulations! You've created a tape labyrinth (Figure 6.2g). To use this method to make an outdoor permanent labyrinth from stone or other markers, set a stone down wherever you might have placed tape, and connect the marker stones with other stones to complete the circuits.

MAKING A CRETAN LABYRINTH
WITH ROPE

This method teaches you how to make a temporary outdoor labyrinth from rope and stakes. Once you've gathered your labyrinth materials, you can take them with you to a park, schoolyard, or public outdoor space for a temporary labyrinth. For easy reference, photocopy the figures used to construct the labyrinth, and cover the photocopies with clear self-adhesive paper for durability in outside use.

Materials

- Approximately 450 feet of rope for a labyrinth with two-foot-wide paths. Buy 500 feet of rope so you don't run out midconstruction.
- One hundred wooden garden stakes to mark where you will lay the ropes down to create the path walls. If you can't find wooden stakes, buy tongue depressors or craft sticks.
- Permanent marker to mark numbers and letters on the wooden stakes.
- Measuring rope: cut a length of the rope two feet longer than eight times the planned width of the paths. For instance, if you are creating a labyrinth with two-foot-wide paths, cut a length of rope eighteen feet.
- Guide stake for the measuring rope. A round wooden dowel works best.
- Duffel (optional) to store the materials for future labyrinths.

You will begin by creating an "outline" of the labyrinth on the ground with numbered wooden stakes in the same manner as you used pieces of tape in the previous labyrinth. You will then lay down two ropes around the stakes to create this labyrinth just as you joined the pieces of tape with longer pieces of tape to create the labyrinth above.

Instructions

1. Refer to Figure 6.3a. The numbers represent the walls of the circuits. The letters are drawn at the four dots of the original seed pattern, along with the number of the circuit they are on (2A, 6B, 7C, and 3D). Notice that D is not directly under C as in the original seed pattern, but one

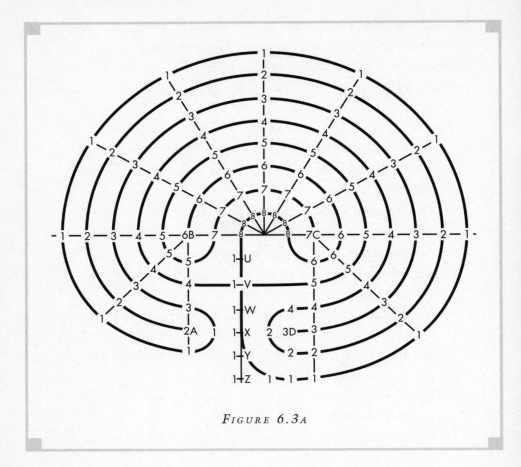

Figure 6.3A

path width to the right of its original placement to allow for
an expanded center.

2. Lay out the wooden stakes. With the permanent marker,
write a number or letter on the tip of each one as follows:

- Fourteen stakes with 1
- One stake with 1U
- One stake with 1V
- One stake with 1W
- One stake with 1X
- One stake with 1Y
- One stake with 1Z

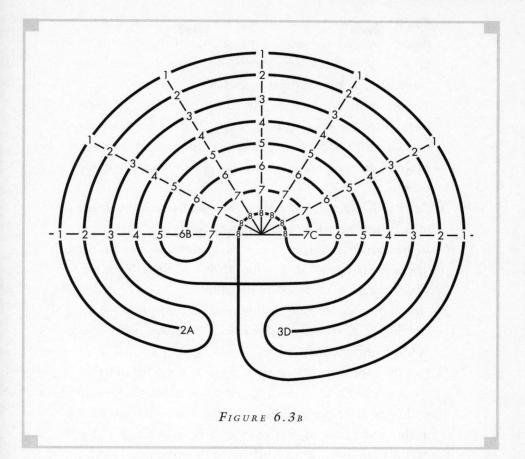

FIGURE 6.3B

- Twelve stakes with 2
- One stake with 2A
- Eleven stakes with 3
- One stake with 3D
- Twelve stakes with 4
- Eleven stakes with 5
- Eight stakes with 6
- One stake with 6B
- Six stakes with 7
- One stake with 7C
- Seven stakes with 8

You'll have several stakes left over for extras as needed in the future. Separate the stakes into bundles of the same numbers to keep track of them. When you dismantle the labyrinth, you can tie them in groups for future use.

3. Tie one end of the measuring rope to the dowel, loosely enough for the rope to pivot freely. Make a mark on the rope one path width from where the rope leaves the dowel. Make seven more marks on the rope, each the width of one path.

4. Refer to figure 6.3b for steps 4 through 9. Push the dowel into the ground where you'd like the center of the labyrinth to be, which will not be the geometrical center of the labyrinth. (Remember, the top "half" of the labyrinth is slightly larger than the bottom "half.")

   As in the tape labyrinth, you'll create the top "half" of the labyrinth first, making half circles. Place the half circles opposite the entrance.

5. Pull the rope straight and lay it down at the bottom left of the upper half circle. Push a stake marked 8 into the ground at the first rope mark to the left of the dowel. Place stake 7 in the ground at the next mark out. Place stake 6B at the next marker moving out from center, 5 at the next mark, 4 at the next, and so on until you place 1 at the last mark on the rope.

6. Pivot the rope clockwise until it is at a right angle to the line you just created, marking a vertical axis for the half circle. Repeat the staking beginning with stake 8 at the first mark and continuing to stake 1 at the last mark on the rope.

7. Pivot the rope clockwise until it makes a straight line with your first set of markers and is at a right angle to the second set of markers. Repeat the staking process beginning with a stake 8. Place stake 7C into the ground instead of a plain 7.

   Now fill in these three lines with four more lines of stakes radiating out from the center dowel.

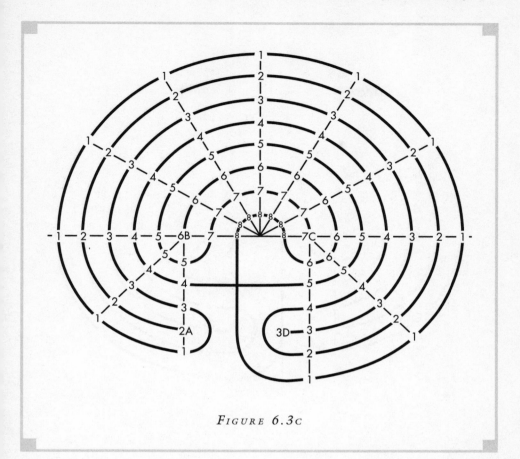

Figure 6.3c

8. Lay the rope straight approximately one-third of the distance between the horizontal line of stakes to the left of center and the vertical line of stakes. Mark the line as before, beginning with stake 8 at the mark closest to the dowel. Pivot the rope another third of the distance between the horizontal and vertical line of stakes, and repeat the staking.

9. Repeat step 8 on the right half of the semicircle, making two lines of stakes each approximately one-third of the distance between the vertical line of stakes and the horizontal line of stakes to the right of center.

Compare your work to Figure 6.3b. You should now have

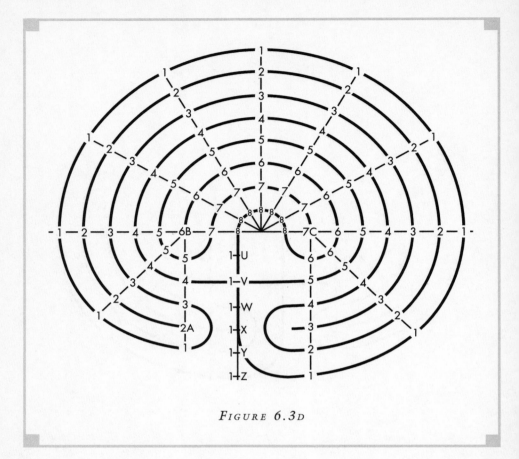

FIGURE 6.3D

eight concentric half circles delineated by seven lines of stakes numbered from 1 at the outside stake of each line to 8 at the innermost stake of each line. You have outlined the top half of your labyrinth.

10. Refer to Figure 6.3c for steps 10 to 13. Take up your guide dowel with the measuring rope still attached. Place the dowel in the ground flush with stake 6B. Lay the rope at a right angle to the horizontal line of stakes of which 6B is a part. Put stake 5 at the first mark from the dowel. Place stake 4 at the next mark and stake 3 at the next. Place stakes 2A and 1 at the next two marks.

11. Pivot the rope halfway between the line of stakes you just created and the horizontal line of stakes above it. Make one more line of stakes, beginning with 5 at the first mark from the dowel and continuing down to 1.

12. Take up the dowel and place it in the ground flush with stake 7C. Lay the rope at a right angle to the horizontal line of stakes of which 7C is a part. Put stake 6 at the first mark from the dowel and place stakes 5 through 1 at the next five marks.

13. Pivot the rope halfway between the line of stakes you just created and the horizontal line of stakes above it. Place stakes 6 through 1.

14. Turn to Figure 6.3d. Reposition the dowel flush with the stake 8 directly left of center. Lay the rope at a right angle to the horizontal line of stakes that runs through stake 8. Place stake 1U at the first marker from the dowel, stake 1V at the second, 1W at the third, 1X at the fourth, 1Y at the fifth, and 1Z at the sixth.

15. Refer back to Figure 6.3a for steps 15 to 19. Pull the measuring rope down to the left and around the bottom of stake 1W so that the rope is going to the right of stake 1W. The third mark from stake 1W should now touch a stake 4. Place another stake 4 at the second knot from where the rope turns at stake 1W. Return the rope to the vertical line of 1U to 1Z.

16. Place the rope to the left and around the bottom of stake 1X so that it is going to the right of stake 1X. The third mark from stake 1X should touch a stake 3. Place stake 3D at the second mark from where the rope turns at stake 1X. Place stake 2 at the first mark from stake 1X. Return the rope to the vertical line of 1U to 1Z.

17. Place the rope to the right and around the bottom of stake 1X so that it is going to the left of stake 1X. The second mark from stake 1X should touch stake 2A. Place stake 1 at

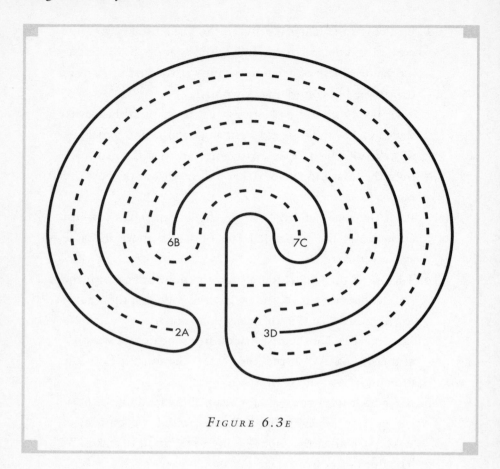

FIGURE 6.3E

the first mark to the left of stake 1X. Return the rope to the vertical line of 1U to 1Z.

18. Place the rope to the left and around the bottom of stake 1Y so that it is going to the right of stake 1Y. The third mark from stake 1Y should touch a stake 2. Place another stake 2 at the second mark to the right of stake 1Y. Return the rope to the vertical line of 1U to 1Z.

19. Place the rope to the left and around the bottom of stake 1Z so that it is going to the right of stake 1Z. The third mark from stake 1Z should touch a stake 1. Place another stake 1 at the second mark to the right of stake 1Z, and one

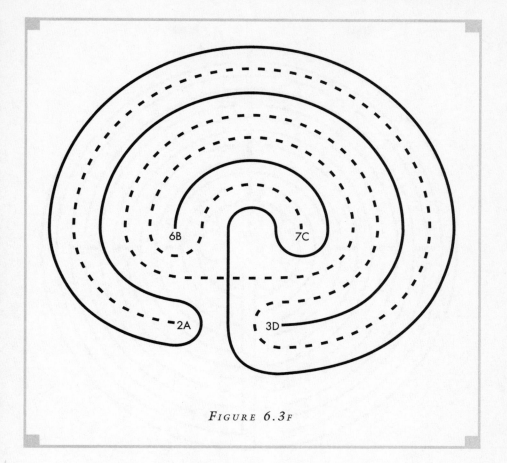

Figure 6.3f

final stake 1 at the first mark from 1Z. Remove the measuring dowel and rope.

All of the numbered stakes of Figure 6.3a should now be in place. Congratulations!

20. Refer to Figure 6.3e. Take the long rope and place one end at stake 6B. Lay the rope down in the curving pattern of the solid line in the figure using the stakes for guides, until you come to stake 3D. Cut the rope to end at stake 3D.

21. Refer to Figure 6.3f. Place the end of the remaining rope at stake 2A. Lay the rope down in the curving pattern of the solid line in the figure using the stakes for guides. When you reach stake 7C, you're done! Cut the rope to end at 7C.

FIGURE 6.4A

Take a moment to admire your handiwork. Remove the wooden stakes and celebrate!

MAKING A CHARTRES LABYRINTH

This simplified form of the Chartres labyrinth (see Figure 6.4a) was developed by Ed Smith, a labyrinth builder who completed a master's degree on the history of the labyrinth. The "lunations," or series of crescents along the rim of the labyrinth, have been omitted and the entrance path shifted slightly to allow ease of construction. (For instructions on how to create a more exact replica of the Chartres labyrinth, see the appendix.)

Notice that one of the primary ways the Chartres labyrinth differs from the Cretan is that the center of the Chartres labyrinth is exactly in the center of the circle, unlike that of the Cretan labyrinth, which is off center.

The instructions here are for a temporary Chartres labyrinth made with masking tape. Since this labyrinth has more circuits than the Cretan one, more space is required. The Chartres labyrinth you will be creating is actually 28 circuits in diameter, allowing for the space in the center. The narrowest usable width for a circuit is one foot; with one-foot paths, at least 30 feet (including a foot around the perimeter) is needed.

Materials

- Thirteen large rolls of one-inch wide masking or electrical tape for a labyrinth with a thirty-foot diameter.
- Measuring rope or string the width of fourteen paths. If you are making a labyrinth with two-foot-wide paths, for instance, you would need a twenty-eight-foot rope.
- Two lengths of string, each the diameter of the labyrinth to be constructed.
- Permanent marker to mark the measuring rope.
- Plumber's plunger for holding the measuring rope in place.
- Music to play during construction to help you relax and concentrate (optional).

Instructions

1. Decide on the size of your labyrinth. Make sure to allow at least one foot of extra space all around the perimeter. Divide the diameter of your usable space by 28; this will be the width of each path. For ease of measurement, round this

Figure 6.4a

down to a whole number. In these instructions, the width of the path will be called W; for instance, if your paths are two feet wide, throughout these instructions W always equals two feet.

2. Tie the measuring rope to the plunger. Measure three times W from the knot and make a mark. This first length delineates the center space. Now make eleven more marks on the rope each W apart.

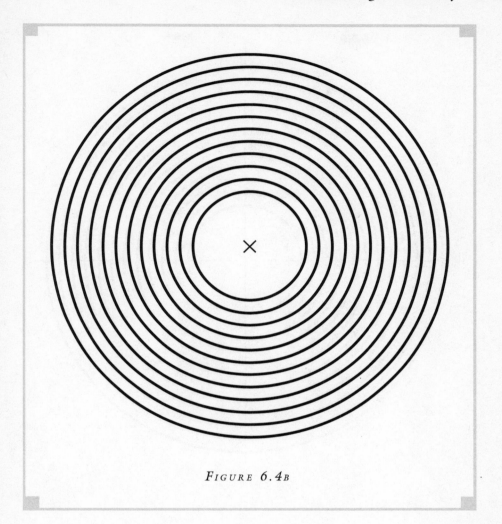

FIGURE 6.4B

3. Refer to Figure 6.4b for steps 3 and 4. Measure your space and find the center. Mark the center of the labyrinth-to-be with a small piece of tape. Tape the plunger over the center (X) with tape.

4. Lay the tape down in twelve concentric circles corresponding to the twelve marks on the measuring rope, pivoting the measuring rope and unrolling the tape as you move the rope around each circle. When you have completed the

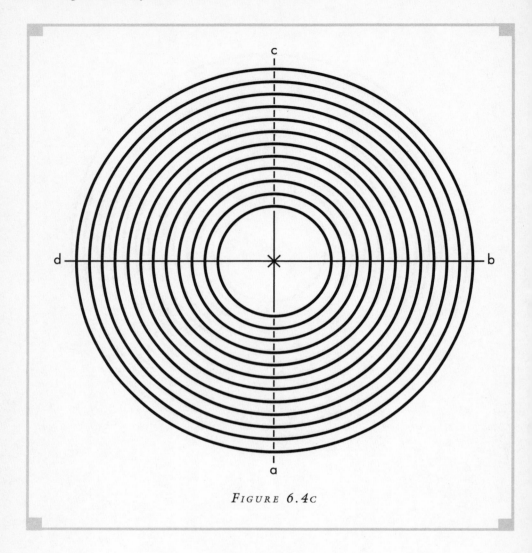

c

d ———————————×——————————— b

a

FIGURE 6.4C

circles, you should have a circular space in the center and 11 concentric paths between 12 lines.

5. Refer to Figure 6.4c. Take the two lengths of string and divide the space for the labyrinth into quadrants. Place the first string with its center over the tape center of the labyrinth. Place the second string at right angles to the first, with its center also over the center mark. Tape the pieces of

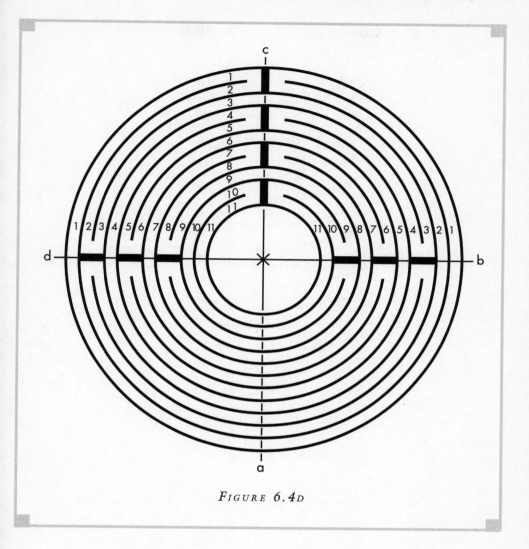

Figure 6.4d

string down in the center and at the outside. Stand back and "eyeball" the strings to make sure they divide the space into four equal quadrants. Notice that letters A to D are assigned to the four ends, or points, of the string. End A marks the eventual entrance to the labyrinth.

6. Refer to Figure 6.4d. Starting from quadrant point B, obstruct the third and fourth paths from point B by putting a piece of tape under the string the width of both paths.

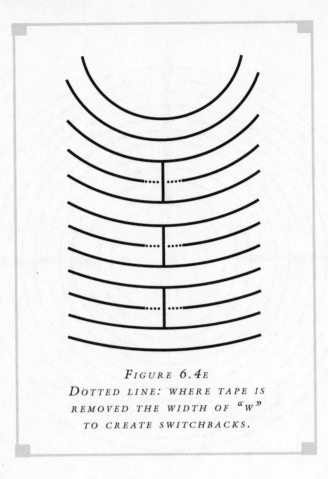

FIGURE 6.4E
DOTTED LINE: WHERE TAPE IS
REMOVED THE WIDTH OF "W"
TO CREATE SWITCHBACKS.

Repeat with the sixth and seventh paths and with the ninth and tenth paths.

7. Refer to Figure 6.4e. Remove the tape separating paths 3 and 4 a distance equal to W. This will create a switch-back, allowing walkers to make a 180-degree turn. Repeat this between paths 6 and 7 and between paths 9 and 10.

Stand back and compare your work to Figure 6.4d. From point B, paths 1 and 2 should be unobstructed. Paths 3 and 4 should be switchbacks. Path 5 should be unobstructed while paths 6 and 7 should be switchbacks. Path 8 should be unobstructed while 9 and 10 are switchbacks. Path 11 should be unobstructed.

8. Refer again to Figure 6.4d. Move counterclockwise to quadrant point C. Obstruct paths 1 and 2 from point C with a piece of tape under the string the width of both paths. Repeat with paths 4 and 5, paths 7 and 8, and paths 10 and 11.

9. Refer back to Figure 6.4e. Remove the tape separating paths 1 and 2 a distance equal to W. This will create a switchback, allowing walkers to make a 180-degree turn. Repeat this between paths 4 and 5, between paths 7 and 8, and between paths 10 and 11.

Stand back and compare your work to Figure 6.4d. From point C, paths 1 and 2 should be switchbacks. Path 3 should be unobstructed while paths 4 and 5 should be switchbacks. Path 6 should be unobstructed while 7 and 8 are switchbacks. Path 9 should be unobstructed while paths 10 and 11 are switchbacks.

10. Refer to Figure 6.4d again. Move counterclockwise to quadrant point D. Obstruct paths 2 and 3 from point D with a piece of tape under the string the width of both paths. Repeat with the fifth and sixth paths, and with the eighth and ninth paths.

11. Refer back to Figure 6.4e. Remove the tape separating paths 2 and 3 a distance equal to W. This will create a switchback, allowing walkers to make a 180-degree turn. Repeat this between paths 5 and 6 and between paths 8 and 9.

Stand back and compare your work to Figure 6.4d. From point D, path 1 should be unobstructed. Paths 2 and 3 should be switchbacks. Path 4 should be unobstructed while paths 5 and 6 should be switchbacks. Path 7 should be unobstructed while paths 8 and 9 are switchbacks. Paths 10 and 11 should be unobstructed.

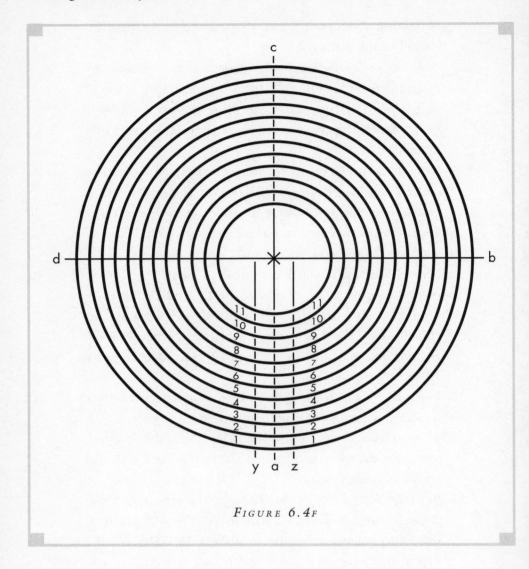

FIGURE 6.4F

12. Refer to Figure 6.4f for steps 12 and 13. Move counter-clockwise to quadrant point A. You will now construct the entrance. Lay a piece of tape from the outermost circle to the innermost circle under quadrant string A. This will be referred to as tape A.

13. Moving to the left of tape A, lay a line of tape parallel to the ver-

"y" "a" "z"

FIGURE 6.4G

tical line of tape you just laid down, the width of W between the two lines of tape. This second line of tape will be called tape Y.

14. NOTE: For steps 14 to 20, refer to Figure 6.4g. Remove the tape from the outermost circle between tape Y and tape A, creating the entrance. Remove the tape in the same manner from the lines between paths 1 and 2, 2 and 3, 3 and 4, and 4 and 5, creating a vertical path.

15. Remove tape Y from path 5, creating the first left turn into the labyrinth.

16. Remove tape Y from path 6.

17. Remove the tape between tape Y and tape A between paths 6 and 7, 7 and 8, 8 and 9, 9 and 10, and 10 and 11, creating another vertical path.

18. Remove tape Y from path 11, creating a left turn into path 11, the centermost path.

    Take a deep breath! You are almost halfway finished with this section.

19. Return to the perimeter. Two pairs of pathways, paths 1 and 2 and paths 3 and 4, to the left of tape Y, will be switchbacks. Starting from the left of tape Y, remove the tape between paths 1 and 2 the width of W. Refer back to Figure 6.4e if needed. Remove the tape between paths 3 and 4 the width of W as well. This will create the switchbacks for paths 1 and 2 and 3 and 4.

20. From the left of tape Y, remove the tape the width of W from between paths 7 and 8 and between paths 9 and 10 to create switchbacks. Now stand back. You should see a total of four switchbacks to the left of tape Y. Compare your labyrinth to Figure 6.4g for accuracy.

    You have now completed the left vertical access paths.

21. Refer to Figure 6.4f. Moving to the right of tape A, lay a line of tape parallel and to the right of tape A, the width of W between the two lines of tape. This second line of tape will be called tape Z.

22. NOTE: For Steps 23 to 26, refer to Figure 6.4g. Remove tape Z from path 1.

23. Remove the tape between tape A and tape Z from the lines between paths 1 and 2, 2 and 3, 3 and 4, 4 and 5, and 5 and 6, creating a vertical path.

24. Remove tape Z from paths 6 and 7.

25. Remove the tape between tape A and tape Z from paths 7

to 11 to create another vertical path leading directly into the center.

26. Return to the perimeter. Four pairs of pathways—paths 2 to 3, 4 to 5, 8 to 9, and 10 to 11—will be switchbacks. From the right of tape Z, remove the tape between paths 2 and 3, 4 and 5, 8 and 9, and 10 and 11 the width of W, referring back to Figure 6.4e if necessary. This will create the switchbacks. Now stand back. You should see a total of four switchbacks to the right of tape Z. Compare this to Figure 6.4g for accuracy.

27. To draw the central rosette, remove the plunger and the measuring rope from the center, leaving the two strings intersecting in the center. With chalk draw the six-petaled flower. Cover the chalk lines with tape.

Congratulations! You have now completed your Chartres labyrinth.

MAKING A LABYRINTH LIGHTLY

"What I want new labyrinth builders to know is that you've got considerable freedom," says Gretchen Schodde. "Get creative and playful. Enjoy yourself. Had I felt when I started creating labyrinths that I had to get the labyrinths technically perfect, I probably never would have created any at all."

Schodde and her volunteer crew adapted the Chartres labyrinth to fit the irregular contours of the land at Harmony Hill, including the sloping roots of the redwood tree around which the labyrinth was designed. "We wanted to honor and accommodate the redwood at the center," recalls Schodde. In addition, they wanted to keep the two small trees that were growing in the outer circuits of the labyrinth. "We moved the string around to widen or narrow the paths in order to incorporate tree roots and the two smaller trees when necessary. Some of the paths are not exactly two feet wide as a result, which means there's a certain irregularity to the whole labyrinth."

Schodde and her crew didn't stick to the recipe. "We listened to what was needed and let go of making a technically 'perfect' labyrinth. What we got in return was a very powerful labyrinth that honored the sacredness of that particular place and the integrity of the trees who were there first. One of the greatest gifts of this labyrinth's irregularity is that it seems to invite people to participate in its continuing evolution. People are always bringing stones and shells to add to its circuits. If this labyrinth had been perfectly laid out, it wouldn't beckon people to participate in its ongoing creation in the same way."

If you want to experiment with different ways of making a labyrinth, go for it! Outside labyrinths have been built irregularly, as at Harmony Hill, to accommodate trees, streams, and boulders. Inside labyrinths have been adapted to rectangular rooms and rooms with supporting pillars.

Remember Jean Lutz's advice about intention, not technical perfection, being the most important ingredient in a labyrinth. Peter Wallis once made a temporary rope labyrinth for a college class. The only room available was quite narrow, and his seven-circuit labyrinth was more rectangular than round.

One of the class participants had been deeply moved the previous year while walking the beautiful labyrinth in the nave of Grace Cathedral in San Francisco. She voiced her doubts to Wallis that the irregular labyrinth could have any effect on walkers, particularly herself. Wallis, having made dozens of temporary labyrinths in many challenging places, encouraged her to walk the labyrinth anyway.

"She had a very moving walk, to her great surprise. She cried all the way through the circuits," Wallis recalls. "It was a lesson for her in looking at how rigid expectations can rob any experience of power."

If you have the interest, aptitude, and right location to make a technically perfect labyrinth, do so. If you're missing one of those "ingredients," go ahead and create a labyrinth anyway. You have nothing to lose. What you have to gain is the powerful experience of creating a transformative tool and the opportunity to then use that tool in any of the ways described in Part Three.

Bon appétit!

CHAPTER SEVEN

Caring for Your Labyrinth

Taking care of the labyrinth you have created is a meditative discipline, much like the careful raking of sand in a Zen temple garden. You may also use the time for creative problem solving or practicing gratitude for the gifts the labyrinth has given you.

One suggestion is to create and care for an altar at the entrance or the center of the labyrinth. Labyrinths invite the conscious placement of altars, or sacred focal points—whether it's a vase of flowers or something more elaborate—by their very design. The center of the labyrinth recalls the heart of a cathedral or Buddhist temple, symbolizing the center of the universe itself. The entrance to the labyrinth represents the threshold between the world of everyday concerns and the world of soul and spirit. Both of the spaces—center and entrance—are powerful places for altars.

ROBERT FERRÉ

A backyard labyrinth in Bad Kreuznach, Germany.

THRESHOLD ALTARS

Recall the spirals that signaled the entrance to sacred space in ancient temples and tombs. Throughout time that threshold between secular and sacred has been marked by statues, altars, curtains, and candles.

Stop, threshold markers tell seekers. *Look; listen. The place you are entering is not ordinary space: It is sacred space. Leave your watches behind: Time here is not clock time,* chronos; *it is* kairos, *the fullness of time beyond time, the eternal Now. Release your daily life and self when you pass this threshold. You are entering sacred ground.*

A threshold altar at the entrance to the labyrinth serves the same purpose: to mark the transition from "hurry" space to sacred space. Before I consciously marked my labyrinth's threshold with a painted stone and a candle, I sometimes found myself—even with the best of intentions to slow down and center—sailing into the circuits planning meeting agendas or making grocery lists. The likelihood of going into the labyrinth unconsciously is greatly lessened when a simple altar at the entrance reminds me that I am entering sacred space. When I lead walks for others, I mark the threshold visually with candles and flowers and aurally by ringing a small bell to signal the next person in line to begin his or her walk.

Take some time now and think about what objects might remind you at the labyrinth threshold that you are entering sacred space. Here are some suggestions:

- A favorite stone or shell.
- A candle you can light before beginning your walk. Small votive candles in glass holders have a better chance of staying lit if your labyrinth is outside. You may have a favorite candleholder you can use, or pick out a special one for the labyrinth threshold.
- A word or symbol that reminds you of what walking the labyrinth means to you. I have painted a stone with the words "Remember and Know" and placed it at the entrance to my labyrinth. I am grateful for these words to Sandra Sarr; I once participated in a walk she facilitated where she whispered these words to each participant as he or she crossed the threshold into the labyrinth.
- A small plant you can tend, either in a pot or planted by the entrance.
- A vase of seasonal flowers or greens.
- A statue or picture of a favorite saint, god/goddess, or animal.

You may place any of these objects on a small table or on the ground, arranging them in a way that is visually pleasing. What is most important is that they remind you that the labyrinth is not business as usual. I find it particularly helpful, given my own tendency to barrel through life, if the altar invites me to stop, light a candle, touch a statue, smell roses. By smelling, touching, lighting, I become more grounded in my own body and the present moment and thus more receptive to Spirit.

Stopping at the entrance altar also helps me focus my intention.

While lighting a candle I can pray for the light of God to illuminate a place of darkness—grief, anger, despair—that I am walking into. Lighting that same candle another time may signify a particular joy or blessing that I am celebrating on the walk: a new job, a completed piece of writing, a healed friendship.

Seeing the words "Remember and Know" at the entrance to my labyrinth invites me to slow down and ask "What is most important to remember this moment, at the beginning of this particular walk?" In times of confusion I have taken the words on that stone with me into the labyrinth, asking myself "Below all this confusion and anxiety, what do I really know, right now? What is vital to remember about myself, about the ones I love, about God, about the very nature of life itself?"

Before exiting the labyrinth, stopping at the threshold altar allows me to ponder the walk for a moment and give thanks. Extinguishing the candle, touching the stone or statue, stroking the soft redness of a rose can help me recross the threshold, making the transition back to everyday space and time.

CENTER ALTAR

An altar at the center of the labyrinth honors the symbolic meaning and power of "the center," reminding us of that still point deep within our souls where we can know the truth.

Sometimes we may need emptiness in the center of the labyrinth, a pregnant void. At other times a simple altar is called for on which we can place icons or statues of the Sacred, a ceramic egg to symbolize new life, a photograph of someone we walk and pray for, blank paper or unshaped clay representing a new creative project.

I love candles in the center altar; for me their flames evoke the light and love of the Sacred. You can light a center candle in one of two ways. You may perform what Gretchen Schodde, director of Harmony Hill, calls "the Short Walk": Before beginning the walk proper, go directly to the center and light the candle as a prelude to the walk;

A rooftop view of Prairie Labyrinth after the routine yearly prairie burn.

then go back to the entrance and walk the labyrinth, thus walking metaphorically toward the Light. Or you may light the candle when you reach the center in the course of your walk, in recognition of that Light.

If you choose, say a brief prayer when you light the candle. Depending on the purpose of the walk, the prayer can ask for the light of healing for yourself or someone else; for the light of understanding in a difficult situation; in gratitude for a birth literal or symbolic; to be a bearer of the light for others; to recognize that same light in all you meet. Lighting a candle is a rich symbolic action, one that can be adapted to almost any sort of intention you might carry into a labyrinth walk.

The central altar is a wonderful place to highlight seasonal symbols. These symbols not only connect us more deeply with the earth and its cycle of seasons, but they also serve to remind us of the inevitability of change, the necessity to embrace the great cycles of life, death, and rebirth, not just in the earth around us but in our own souls and lives.

I put wooden eggs in the center of my labyrinth in spring as a symbol of new beginnings and new life. For Summer Solstice as I wrote this book, I gathered St.-John's-wort, a flowering herb traditionally connected to the solstice. I made a wreath of the sunny yellow blossoms, a circle of light and sunshine, and we carried it into the center of the labyrinth as part of a community Summer Solstice walk.

In the fall I place symbols of whatever I am harvesting in my life to remind me to be grateful; in winter (as Northwest weather permits!) I light as many candles as possible to remind me of the rebirth of the Light. The possibilities for seasonal altars are circumscribed only by your imagination.

If you share your labyrinth with others, wonderful possibilities exist for creating communal altars that reflect the richness and diversity of community. The redwood growing in the center of the labyrinth at Harmony Hill is an important part of that labyrinth's central altar. Candles are lit and flowers placed at its base; over time people have brought small offerings, such as stones, shells, sequin suns, and angels. Walkers over the years have decorated the shaggy crevices of the redwood's bark with small stone hearts, coins, flowers, a pair of silver Celtic knot earrings, a prayer necklace.

Experiment with placing favorite rocks, shells, statues, and icons on the center altar. Give yourself permission to play with different objects and their placement. This need not be deadly serious business; one time when I really needed to lighten up and take myself less seriously I put a pair of Groucho Marx glasses at the base of the redwood in Harmony Hill's labyrinth.

Give yourself permission to experiment with your labyrinth altars. We can get far too serious, losing any flexibility or creativity and shutting out the possibilities for grace so inherent in the altars themselves. As you plan your altar, allow yourself to move into play space; invite the spirit of the child within you out to play!

Here are some questions to help you set up your central altar:

- What objects most powerfully evoke for me the symbolism of Center?

- What objects remind me of the Sacred, of my own higher self?
- What am I working on spiritually right now? What object might remind me of that? (One of my favorite things to place on either altar is a small ceramic replica of an open hand, teaching me about receptivity, openness, and surrender.)

FINGER LABYRINTH ALTAR

If you have made or bought a finger labyrinth, you can experiment with altars there as well. My finger board is the centerpiece of a tabletop altar. Candles flank the miniature labyrinth; a cast of my daughter's open preschool hands graces its entrance, reminding me of the importance of entering the labyrinth, no matter what its size, empty-handed and openhearted.

Besides these basic components, the finger board altar changes with the seasons and with my intentions. I put arrangements of seasonal flowers and greens on the altar. I add more candles at Winter Solstice, eggs at Spring Equinox, a tiny ceramic box my daughter made for me one Mother's Day.

I have placed the labyrinth altar between the kitchen and the entrance to my therapy/writing studio in a separate wing of the house, marking the boundary between my home and my "work." When I go from washing dishes to writing, passing the altar helps me be mindful of the transition. When I move from a full day of seeing clients back to being mother and householder, the altar reminds me of that as sacred work too.

Clients sitting in the waiting area can see the altar, especially if I have lit candles. They know they can trace the labyrinth while they are waiting for their session. Both the altar and the labyrinth at its center remind them that therapy is sacred work.

When I use my finger labyrinth, I like to light the candles on the altar before beginning, saying a prayer just as I do at my outside labyrinth. I then either trace the finger board as I stand in front of it or take it to a comfortable chair if I need more time. When I am done with the journey, I replace the labyrinth, say a prayer of gratitude, and extinguish the candles.

MAINTAINING THE LABYRINTH

L ate afternoon in the city. With the faint roar of the freeway at my back, I stop for a moment at the entrance to my labyrinth to see what needs to be done. This is not walking time; it is grooming time. I notice that the rope which delineates the labyrinth's circuits is becoming entangled by overgrown grass, so I spend the next forty-five minutes gently pulling it out from the thatch. As I work, I contemplate how I allow the presence of Spirit in my life to become obscured by the overgrowth of day-to-day details. The roar of traffic recedes; body and soul tune instead to the cadences of the creek that runs nearby, the breeze in the cottonwoods overhead. I am restored, as the labyrinth is restored.

"There's no such thing as a labyrinth that doesn't require maintenance!" asserts Sig Lonegren, author of *Labyrinths: Ancient Myths and Modern Uses.* "The question then becomes, 'How can I integrate maintenance of my labyrinth into my spiritual path?' Just because you're weeding your labyrinth or straightening rocks doesn't mean your mind and your spirit can't be doing something. If you look at maintenance as a creative spiritual activity, I think it's actually more powerful than walking."

Toby Evans, creator of the Prairie Labyrinth, agrees. Evans has created a majestic 166-foot-wide labyrinth on her property, mown out of native prairie grasses she sowed with the help of the Prairie Restoration Project. The Prairie Labyrinth is high maintenance, as stray grasses—eight feet high by midsummer—fall over daily into the path, particularly after a high wind or rain. Evans has to hand-prune these strays as well as mow the labyrinth path with her riding mower, but she doesn't begrudge the maintenance time. "Maintenance is my communion, my church. For me, it's not the meditation walk, it's the maintenance meditation. I go into the labyrinth and with the maintenance work out every issue that's coming up in my life. Caring for the labyrinth has altered my life; it's what has most rearranged me, my thinking, my spirit, you name it. The benefit others get is from walking. For me, it's in the taking care of this labyrinth."

One of my favorite ways to recenter at Harmony Hill amid the intensity of writing or leading a retreat is to weed the dark gravel that forms the paths or straighten the oyster shells delineating them. By pulling crabgrass or realigning shells I can say thank-you to the labyrinth for all that it has given me. Giving my sweat and my time is a way of expressing gratitude for this powerful vehicle for Spirit in the physical world.

"Responding to the needs of the labyrinth is my personal pilgrimage," says Cielle Tewksbury, who tends a labyrinth on her property in Vermont. "I can embody my gratitude by attending to the labyrinth. I had expected that its presence as a walking meditation would be its paramount reward. I have learned that it is not the daily walking but the daily attending that is its richest gift."

Your labyrinth, however it is constructed, will need your care and maintenance. Labyrinths in yards need mowing, raking, weeding. Stone labyrinths need realigning. Even canvas labyrinths need cleaning, and finger boards dusting.

MAINTENANCE GIFTS

Weeding, raking, and cleaning the labyrinth can yield the same gifts as walking. A powerful way to play with labyrinth caretaking is to bring an intention with you into caretaking, as you would with walking. Acknowledge your intention at the entrance to the labyrinth, walk in, and begin grooming it, remaining open for, as Sig Lonegren calls them, "daysigns." "Think of whatever you see or deal with while maintaining the labyrinth as a 'daysign,' the way dream symbols are 'nightsigns.' If you come upon a dandelion," explains

Lonegren, "play with that every way you can. What does 'lion' have to do with what you're thinking about as you take care of your labyrinth? What does yellow have to do with it? Play with it! Think about the dandelion's medicinal aspects and what that might be saying to you about the issue at hand.

"Or say you're thinking about your kid, who's in trouble, while you're maintaining your labyrinth. You're wondering how to deal with your child, and you look up and see an owl flying over you. You think 'wisdom,' and realize you need to go talk to your child's teacher, who is wise and a friend of yours.

"Look for daysigns as you take care of your labyrinth: animals, plants, the wind and weather, 'chance' occurrences or coincidences that take place while you're weeding or sweeping. Be open to their symbolism and what they have to teach you about the issues in your life."

Maintaining an outside labyrinth also connects the caretaker more deeply with the rhythms and cycles of nature, by deeply and mindfully connecting with one particular place throughout the year. "Through maintaining the labyrinth, there's a deepening with nature itself," says Toby Evans. "I have never so totally immersed myself in nature as I have taking care of the labyrinth. I feel like I'm becoming the grasses as they grow through the spring and summer—I've gotten to know the personalities of the different kinds of grasses, the very different feel of each one. The labyrinth is really alive, constantly transforming with the cycles of nature. Every day I feel like I've entered a new place. The labyrinth changes so drastically with each season: so tall in summer, so flat in winter."

Cielle Tewksbury imagines the grasses she must cut every day as current life challenges or as parts of her own self that need attention. "Through maintenance, I've done more shadow work than in any other way in my life," she explains. "I meet parts of myself that I wouldn't meet elsewhere. It forces unacknowledged and undealt-with stuff up by physically having to do the kind of work involved in taking care of a labyrinth. This particular thing is in your way; how is it like a challenge or obstacle you're facing right now? . . . I have learned that it is not the daily walking but the daily attending that is the labyrinth's richest gift."

LABYRINTH EVOLUTION

Just as seasons change, so may your labyrinth. You might find that the structure itself needs to be modified in order to make maintenance easier. Sig Lonegren originally lined his labyrinth paths with sand. Over time, and through much weeding, he decided to change the composition of the paths from sand to bark chips. He now has covered the paths with bark and—to his great delight—has found that the amount of time spent weeding has dropped significantly.

As you work with your labyrinth over time, you may want to change certain physical aspects of it for personal or aesthetic reasons. Cedar kindling originally lined the paths on the Chartres labyrinth at Harmony Hill; over the years stones brought by guests and workshop participants replaced some of the kindling and added to the richness of the circuits. I felt especially drawn to the oyster shells from the Hood Canal beach next to Harmony Hill that someone added to the circuits, both aesthetically for the white pearliness against the darkness of the charcoal gray gravel, but also for the shells symbolizing that Harmony Hill was on water renowned for its fecundity. How wonderful it would be, I thought, to have a labyrinth that honored the particular genius of this bioregion, by lining it completely with oyster shells rather than river stones.

Someone else had already brought up some shells from the canal to put in the labyrinth. I finished that bucket, went down to the beach with an armful of plastic bags to fill with more shells, and the project was born.

Groups at Harmony Hill, from women from the local women's prison, to cancer retreats, to theological study groups, have helped with the project, bringing more oyster shells up from the beach and slowly replacing the cedar. This labyrinth is alive, not just from its connection to the particular piece of earth it graces but from the love and goodwill of all those who have cared for it and helped it evolve.

Labyrinths are not inert collections of stones, rope, or tape. You will find as you work with your labyrinth, no matter what its size or composition, that it has a certain living quality to it.

Just like a living being, the labyrinth responds to your care. After I spend time grooming a labyrinth, the air feels clearer within its circuits, the colors brighter, the energy freer. What I find, as you will as well, is that it is not just the labyrinth that benefits from this loving care. After spending time caring for the labyrinth, I too feel cleaner, lighter, more connected to my own body and soul.

Part Three

Playing and Healing with the Labyrinth

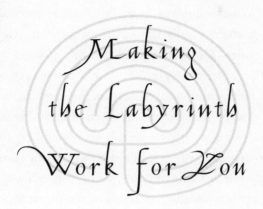

CHAPTER EIGHT

Making the Labyrinth Work for You

OU MUST BE PRESENT IN ORDER TO WIN ran an old bingo sign that I once had hanging on the wall of my office. I wish I still had the sign to show participants at the labyrinth workshops I lead.

The labyrinth invites us to show up. Our best response to this powerful invitation is mindful preparation for a walk. The more consciously we prepare for the walk, the deeper and more transformative that walk will be.

Preparation can be a simple matter of taking a moment to stand at the entrance to the labyrinth, breathing and becoming clear about our intentions for walking. Preparation may also mean several days of thoughtful rumination as we get ready for a labyrinth retreat.

THE POWER OF CONSCIOUS INTENTION

By being fully conscious of our intentions for any particular walk, we harness the power of the labyrinth. We can frame those intentions as either a question or a statement; the power of the intention is not in how it is worded but in that it is consciously chosen and walked into.

We must also be willing to hear the truth as we walk into our intention. Sig Lonegren calls the labyrinth a "hermetic tool." He claims that Hermes, Greek messenger to the gods, is a powerful archetype for the labyrinth. "Hermes, as the messenger of the gods, goes back and forth from the physical to the spiritual realms," says Lonegren. "Whatever your intention, when you send it out, Hermes brings back the message. It's important to remember, though, that Hermes is also the god of liars. This means you'll sometimes get bogus answers while walking the labyrinth. You can ask a question and have such a powerful subconscious need for a particular response that you can't hear anything else. If that's the case, that's the response that Hermes will bring you. If you're after the truth, and you want Hermes to bring you the truth, you've got to put aside that need for a specific answer."

I have learned the painful way about meeting Hermes halfheart-edly. I remember one walk when I wanted to know what to do about a friendship that had become quite difficult. I was clear at the beginning of the walk that I wanted guidance on how to help untangle it. However, as I walked I became even more confused about what I could do to help heal the relationship. When the walk ended, I was enormously frustrated and feeling even more resentful about the state of the friendship.

I had to spend some time thinking about what went wrong, given that I usually ended a walk with more, rather than less, clarity on whatever issue I had taken in. I realized that, although I had been clear about wanting a solution, I hadn't been entirely honest: I really wanted *her* to solve it, not wanting to take responsibility for my contribution to the mess we were in.

Because I was still in blaming mode and not being honest with myself, I wasn't ready for any guidance to come through. I didn't want to hear *anything* other than confirmation that I was right and she was wrong. Of course, no guidance had come through to support my self-righteous position. I returned to the labyrinth, this time being clear that I was willing to receive guidance that might challenge my entrenched position.

I walked and was challenged in a loving way. I became clearer about my part in the creation and maintenance of our difficulties. At the center I prayed again for help in healing the relationship and got clarity on the way out for how I could initiate some healing. What made all the difference between the two walks was my willingness in the second to hear the truth even if it meant getting shaken up a bit.

After that experience I have learned to ask myself while formulating an intention "Am I really willing to know what I know? Am I really willing to receive guidance that may lead me in a new direction? Is my commitment to knowing the truth greater than my commitment to having the answer be the one I'm demanding?"

If I can honestly say yes, then I proceed with the walk. If, however, I get a sense that I'm unwilling to have anything but a particular answer, then it's time to compassionately acknowledge my fear and unwillingness to go deeper into the truth of whatever the issue is. I then have a choice: I can either pick a different intention for the walk, or I can have as my intention to walk more deeply into the fear or anxiety of the resistance and see where that takes me. Either choice is fine. What is important is that the choice be made consciously.

Remember the acronym GIGO—garbage in, garbage out? If we go into a walk determined to hear only one answer, that's the answer we'll get, whether it's the truth for us or not. The more willing we are to hear truth, the greater the chances that we will receive guidance that leads us to greater healing and wholeness.

FRAMING INTENTIONS AND QUESTIONS

To begin your walk, think of a question or issue that concerns you right now, whether mundane or sublime. I have worked with participants, and walked myself, with issues that range from "Do I really need to buy that outfit?" to struggling with deeper religious issues. What matters most is how much it matters to you, whatever "it" is.

The subject might be glaringly obvious to you: an upcoming job interview, a spiritual issue you're struggling with, a birthday, a fight you had with your partner. If nothing is so pressing or present, ask yourself, "What do I need more clarity on in my life?" "What feels unresolved?" "What does life (or God) seem to be inviting me to learn more about, or deal with, right now?" Breathe into the questions and be open to what comes up; it may be a very familiar issue or one you haven't given much thought to. Pay attention, though, to the energy of the issue or question: If it feels alive and juicy to you, it's a good one to walk with.

Here are some possible intentions:

- Prayers for a particular person or situation. You may pray for someone as you walk or simply hold that person in light and love. You can also use labyrinth time to pray for events, people, or the planet itself.
- The upcoming or past year at a birthday or anniversary. You can use the walk to reflect on the past year or walk into your dreams and goals for the upcoming year. (See Chapter 9.)
- Working with a particular emotion or state: gratitude, grief, confusion, fear, forgiveness. You can walk with a particular feeling, bringing it into sacred space for healing; you can investigate the feeling as you walk, asking for guidance in understanding it better; you can surrender it to Spirit as you walk. (See Chapter 10.)
- A relationship issue. You can walk with a prayer for healing a particular relationship; you can have an intention receiving guidance for helping it to grow; you can walk with the purpose of understanding a particular relationship issue from a "God's-eye view."

- A spiritual question. You can have the walk be a way of understanding or healing a spiritual issue: trust, love, grace. (See Chapter 10.)
- Vocational issues. "What do I want from work?" "Does this job fully engage me and use my strengths and capabilities to my advantage?" You can bring these questions into the labyrinth, and/or ask for help in an upcoming meeting, job interview, or dealing with office politics in a way that has integrity for you.
- A creative project. The labyrinth is a wonderful place to bring a creative project into, walking for guidance on how the project should be unfolding. Walking when you're creative is a very powerful way of dealing with blockages. (See Chapter 9.)
- A particular event and its meaning for you. Momentous events and life transitions—beginnings and endings of relationships, jobs, and school; life phases such as a child leaving home; dreams lost and dreams realized—can be brought into the labyrinth for support, guidance, and understanding. These events can also be worked with ritually in the labyrinth for deeper guidance, support, or celebration. (See Chapter 12.)

After you gain clarity about the issue, think about how you can state it most concisely as an intention or question. Phrase it in a way that allows for the most open-ended exploration and learning. For instance, if you are struggling with resistance to opening up to your partner, you might state "I want to learn more about my resistances to intimacy" rather than "How can I be less resistant?"

You also can phrase your issue as a question. I often prefer to ask questions, remembering that someone once told me that God doesn't ask us to know the answers but to love the questions. Loving a difficult question, such as "How can I allow the sexual abuse I've lived through to be a teacher for me?" through a walk—rather than demanding an answer—allows for a deeper, more reflective part of our minds and hearts to be engaged, which ultimately opens the door for new answers and healing.

You may also work with your intention as an image, or a gesture, or by reducing it to one word. An intention for the healing of the relationship with an estranged friend could be condensed to repeating your friend's name or the word "healing"; holding an image of healing light connecting and surrounding the two of you; or walking with your hands gently touching your heart to invoke healing. If I find I am resisting an uncomfortable issue or a feeling, I walk with my hands open, palms up, before me in a gesture of opening and surrender.

SUPPORTING INTENTION WITH LIGHTING AND MUSIC

What preparation does, though, is to focus mind and heart on walking the labyrinth. I find that the time spent preparing the space is transition time. While setting out candles or checking the altar, I am switching out of "doing" mode and into "being." My mind quiets down; I become more reflective and receptive to guidance and inspiration.

There are many ways to prepare the labyrinth for a solo or group walk: preparing the lighting, setting the stage with sound or music, and preparing the altar.

LIGHTING

The other day, feeling discouraged about a writing project, I went outside to walk the labyrinth. Just before I began I realized I needed something more than just the walk itself; I needed to remember the Light at the center, both of the labyrinth and of my own creative abilities. I returned to my studio and found a small votive candle in a sturdy glass holder. Taking it outside, I stood at the labyrinth's entrance, said a brief prayer for help in remembering my own creative light, and lit the candle. I went straight to the center and placed the votive in the central altar, then walked out directly.

Now I could walk; lighting the candle both slowed me down and centered me for the walk, and gave me a beacon to walk toward. As I circled around the light and finally entered its space, I could reopen to the light within me. I turned to extinguish the candle when I left the center but decided instead to let it burn. I walked out knowing the light was still going and bowed to it briefly before leaving.

For the next hour or so, I glanced up from my studio, where I was writing, to see the small flame giving light to the center of the labyrinth. That flame eased me back into my writing, reminding me to relax and trust the process, knowing that the light was always there within me. Later that afternoon I walked back out to the labyrinth, said a prayer of gratitude at the entrance, and walked directly in. I took the still-burning candle back with me to my desk, leaving a rose in the center of the labyrinth in thanks to Spirit.

There are many creative ways to work with lighting the labyrinth. You may have a single candle at the center, as I did on that walk. You can also light a candle or candles at the entrance and at the four quarters of the labyrinth.

You may use either tapers for candles or votives set in glass containers. I prefer votives; they tend to stay lit longer because their containers keep the wind out. You also can set larger candles in Mason jars to keep them from the wind.

Another option is to set out luminarias, candles set in sand at the bottom of small paper bags, which give off a lovely glow. Take a paper lunch bag and turn down the top edge a half inch, then turn it down a half inch more. This creates stiffness in the bag. Fill the bottom of the bag with about an inch and a half of sand. (You can buy sand at hardware stores in ten-pound bags.) Set the luminarias out in the labyrinth wherever you would like them to be: entrance, center, four quarters. When you are ready for the walk, place small candles securely in the sand and light them.

Luminarias create a beautiful suffused glow for walking. I love using them for night walks and especially for walks around Winter Solstice, when light in the Northwest is so painfully lacking, to remind me and others of the Light we all carry within ourselves even during outer darkness and of the imminent return of the outer light as well.

Sound

Sound, in any of its forms—music, drumming, chanting, bells—may be used both to prepare for the walk and during the walk. Taped music, particularly for indoor labyrinths, can set the mood and tone for a walk. If you are walking outside, you can experiment with using a small cassette or CD player and headphones rather than a larger music system. Reflective, slow music, such as the Pachelbel Canon or a Gregorian chant, can set the stage for a deeply contemplative walk. Musica Divina, an eclectic chamber ensemble that plays music live for labyrinth walks at Grace Cathedral in San Francisco, has recorded music specifically for the purpose. More passionate music, such as Loreena McKennitt's, will set an entirely different mood.

Imagine how different pieces you love might affect the tempo and quality of a labyrinth walk. Feel free to experiment with different kinds of music in the labyrinth, including recordings of drumming or environmental tapes of ocean waves or wind.

One of the most memorable walks I have ever led incorporated both light and music in the preparation. During one menopause retreat I led at Harmony Hill the group decided to walk the labyrinth at night. While the women sat inside listening to a storyteller, Gretchen Schodde and I placed luminarias around the perimeter of the redwood labyrinth, at the entrance, in the center, and in the four directions marked inside the circuits.

When all thirty or so luminarias were lit (no little feat on a gusty night!), Gretchen and I returned to the main house where we all lined up in silence. As we began the walk through the orchard to the labyrinth, one woman beat a cadence with a drum she had just made; another shook a rattle she had created the previous year on a vision quest. Gretchen swung a deep and sonorous cowbell from her childhood farm. As we walked we let the drumming and bell ringing take us deeper and deeper into silence.

The drumming stopped, but the bell continued to toll as we walked the labyrinth, its evocative ringing riding the energy of the increasing wind. I felt the wild dark loneliness of the night evoking the same wildness within me. There was magic in the wind, the candles, the tolling of the bell, the darkness, the community of women.

No one left the area as she finished her walk; the women gathered outside the labyrinth until the last walker came out swinging the bell. We stayed outside linked arm in arm, singing the full moon up through the branches of the redwood at the labyrinth's center. When the moon finally crested the top of the stately tree, we fell once more into silence. The magic of the drum, the bell, the rattle, and the luminarias had attuned us to the magic of the labyrinth and of the deep night.

WALKING WITH INTENTION

Begin your walk with an invocation for guidance and support from that being or principle in whose Light you walk: your Higher Power, a favorite god or goddess, the four directions, a spirit animal. This invocation can be verbal, as in a prayer; visual, bringing to your heart and mind a favorite image; or physical, a deep breath or bow. Acknowledge in your invocation both your intention and your commitment to the truth. When you are ready, step into the labyrinth.

As you walk, let your intention or question sink more deeply into your heart and soul with each step. Responses and intuitions may come in the form of words, feelings, kinesthetic awareness, images, or just knowing. For instance, if your intention was "I want to learn more about my resistances to intimacy," you might see an image of your angry father from childhood; hear the words "Your fear of being left is simply your fear"; find your fists clenching tighter and tighter, along with your jaw; or simply know that this has something to do with the way you were mocked on the playground in fourth grade. The responses may be more cryptic: a bare tree, a stormy ocean, a tight gut. If you get responses you don't understand at first, the center is a good place to ask for additional guidance in understanding. You may also journal about your experience later.

Your attention may wander as you walk, as it does in meditation. As in meditation, if you find yourself thinking about what to bring to the potluck tomorrow night or how to get a loan for that new car, gently bring your heart and mind back to your intention.

Play with being softly aware of your surroundings as you walk into your intention. Just as objects appearing in dreams may have far more symbolic significance than they have in waking life, so may "daysigns" have symbolic information for you about your intention.

I once walked the labyrinth with the intention of learning how to trust myself more. I noticed that several different times I accidentally kicked the river stones forming the walls of the circuits out of place. After I became aware of this, I played gently with its significance as I walked.

I realized that each one of those stones was right in my path, and yet I hadn't seen any of them. Thinking about my own lack of trust in myself, I understood how sometimes I couldn't—or wouldn't—see what was right in front of me, noticing an issue only when it caused me to stumble. Those stones taught me how important it was, in order to trust myself, to walk clear-eyed and awake on my path, so that I could see obstacles coming and have choices about what to do with them rather than stumble, insisting to myself and others I never saw the obstacles coming.

One man at a workshop, walking through the pain of a divorce that was still eating away at his heart and soul after three years, noticed a hawk circling above him as he walked. In his imagination Paul asked the hawk for wisdom about his question of how to heal his bitterness.

"Hawk told me I needed to pull way back from being right inside of my bitterness, stop walking it right into the ground over and over. He invited me to look at all this from his perspective to get a much bigger picture and be able to circle around it from way far off. Part of my bitterness," Paul told me, "was my refusing to see anything but my own hurt and anger. When I got to the center, that hawk was still soaring above me, so I sat down and closed my eyes and let him take me flying. Way up there I could see how tiny the labyrinth looked, how it was just part of a larger picture of fields and houses and trees.

"'Look,' Hawk told me, 'see that little labyrinth down there? See how it's only a piece of a much bigger pattern? The story you tell yourself about your divorce is really that small too, but you keep hanging on to it like it's the whole picture. It isn't—there's your ex-wife's story about the divorce, there's God's story about the divorce, there's the story you'll tell about the divorce on your deathbed when you're a whole lot older and wiser than you are right now.'

"Man, I really listened to what this bird was telling me, because he was right. I was holding on to that bitterness like it was the last thing I had. Seeing everything from this hawk's perspective helped me let go of some of that pain—it just wasn't so important anymore and was keeping me stuck in a very little place. I walked out of that labyrinth a whole lot freer man than the one who walked it, and it was because I paid attention to that bird."

WALKING OPEN-MINDED

J t's important to allow every walk to be an open-minded one. Labyrinth space is not only sacred space; it is magical space as well, where anything can and does happen. "I really think that labyrinths are churners," says Sig Lonegren. Lonegren likens the labyrinth to the cauldron of Celtic goddess Cerridwen, representing the cauldron of death and rebirth, of transformation, of wisdom.

"I see the pattern of the labyrinth as the pattern of Cerridwen stirring her cauldron. When we walk this pattern, it's as if we're both stirring the cauldron and the self is getting stirred at the same time. You know what stirring does—it brings up all the stuff that's settled to the bottom."

When we walk this cauldron-path, "stuff" may get stirred up that we had no idea was there. When that happens, it can be important to go with the stirring, letting go of our original intention.

The first time I walked the redwood labyrinth at Harmony Hill, I was leading a workshop at the retreat house next door. I took the retreatants to Harmony Hill to walk the labyrinths. I waited until everyone had finished walking the redwood labyrinth and decided to walk a "quickie" before dinner by myself, with the intention of opening to guidance about the evening's activities with the group.

Everything went fine until I reached the center and touched the soft fissures in the bark of the redwood. My heart broke wide open in grief over leaving the garden of the house I had just sold. I had grieved about leaving that garden for almost a year, and I assumed the grieving was mostly done. Obviously I was wrong. Reaching the center of the labyrinth and touching the tree had opened a deep well of tears that I thought had run dry.

I knew I had a choice at that point: to return to my original intention of thinking about the after-dinner program or to allow the grief to move through me. I chose the latter, and grieved deeply over leaving a garden that I had created and maintained for more than a decade, a garden that in many ways had been a spiritual path for me. The grief finally crested and subsided. I thanked the redwood for its quiet, caring presence and walked out feeling cleansed, renewed, and deeply at peace.

That evening with the participants was a special one for me. After my experience in the labyrinth, I felt deeply at ease with the process of the group and newly compassionate to the losses that many of the retreatants were dealing with that weekend.

Walking "open-minded" also means releasing expectations for how a walk will be. Not all walks will be life-changing, particularly if you settle into an ongoing relationship with a labyrinth.

Remember my own story? I kept expecting fireworks and kept getting disappointed. I have seen this happen over and over again with others as well. We expect some profound and life-changing insight, and "nothing" happens. We assume we've done something wrong, so the next time we try harder: focus even more on our breath, our mantra, our walk.

The problem isn't that nothing happens during the walk. The problem is that we're clutching a particular expectation for how the walk "should" be. Some of your walks will be prosaic, chances simply to be in the present moment. Just as with any other endeavor in life, while walking the labyrinth there is an X factor composed of such details as the weather, the amount of sleep we had last night, our own physical and emotional health, and, finally, just a good wallop of pure Mystery.

This X factor guarantees we have no ultimate control over the outcome of our walk, just as we have no ultimate control over the outcome of anything in our lives. Hindu thought recognizes this and celebrates the path of Karma yoga, of staying present with what needs to be done while giving up the results to God.

"Get rid of your preconceived notions," advises Jean Lutz of the *Labyrinth Letter*. "Take the labyrinth walk for what it is for you. Don't bring expectations into it. *Get out of your own way!* I see so many people coming to the labyrinth with a certain set of expectations: 'This is the way I'm *supposed* to walk it, this is what I'm *supposed* to get out of it.' It's so sad, because a whole lot of those people are disappointed."

As you develop a "walking relationship" with your labyrinth, you will find that you have amazing experiences. You also will find that sometimes you have walks that are prosaic or even boring. Dry walks, and even a dry series of walks, are like dry times in a relationship or dry times in your creative or spiritual life.

If you find yourself in a fallow walk or in a fallow walking time, keep going. Remember St. Francis's advice that, even if you simply return to your breath the whole time in meditation, it is time well spent. It could be that your intention or prayer is working subsoil, so to speak, and that powerful growth will emerge later as a result. It could be that what you are learning, as in the classic dark night of the soul in spirituality, is trust: trust that Spirit is there and at work in your heart and soul, even if you can discern no visible signs. Walking through fallowness, just as praying through a desert experience, can be a very powerful growth time in retrospect.

Paradoxically, it is only by learning to let go of expectations and outcome in the labyrinth that the most powerful work can happen. When we are trying to have an important insight or heal a relationship, it is our small selves doing the work. If we can let our small selves step aside, letting Spirit take care of the outcome, we are allowing much more powerful forces to gather, forces for healing and grace and life, than we ever could marshal on our own.

Learning to do this in the labyrinth—to not push for a particular feeling, or process, or outcome—has yielded rich rewards in my "other" life as teacher, therapist, mother, partner as well. Walking in the labyrinth without holding on to the outcome reminds me to stay present in my life, showing up fully, and allowing Spirit to take care of the outcome. Letting go of "trying" in the labyrinth helps me to remember to let go of "trying hard" to control other people, the process, and the outcome of all the unfolding events of my life.

Walking with intention has taught me, time and time again, the power of purpose: not just in the labyrinth but in all of my life. Beginning a walk with a clear intention while at the same time keeping an open mind and soft heart for whatever unfolds on the walk teaches me to do the same in the larger walk of my own life.

CHAPTER NINE

Creativity and Intuition

Much of the work and play of this book has been done in the labyrinth, from envisioning the book and inviting spiritual help, to planning individual chapters, editing, dealing with creative blocks, and celebrating small victories.

I have walked the labyrinth specifically asking for help and guidance on the writing of each chapter. After finishing each chapter in rough draft I walk the labyrinth once more, asking "Is there anything else I should be thinking about or writing about in this chapter?" I bring a notebook with me on these walks, as ideas, images, and even important phrases or sentences come to me as I walk or meditate in the center. When I have hit blocks in writing, as you shall see later in this chapter, I have turned to the labyrinth for freeing up my creative juices.

I have also used the labyrinth to envision and plan new classes and workshops, to dream new dreams for my life and work with bringing them into reality, and to deal with internal blocks to inspiration. You also can use the labyrinth to allow more creativity to flow in your own life.

"Creativity? I'm not creative," people tell me all the time. I don't believe it, not for a second.

What I do know, though, is that from an early age we are trained to belittle our own creative efforts. When my friend Rodger was in kindergarten, he was given an "art test" and told that he *flunked* it! Perhaps we were more subtly discouraged, but almost all of us find ourselves creatively challenged from time to time, finding it hard to believe in our own God-given creative gifts.

We are all creative and intuitive. Our creativity and intuition are like a radio signal that is always transmitting from a source deep inside of us. However, early parental messages, school, and our culture overlay a thick band of white noise on that signal. We mistakenly believe we are neither creative nor intuitive, because all we perceive is the static. When we clear out the static we can hear that inner signal, clear and true.

The labyrinth is a powerful way to clear out the static and recover the signal. During walking, the attention is turned inward, the mind is stilled, and everyday concerns are released, creating the perfect setting for creative and intuitive juices to flow. In the labyrinth we have a chance to think radically new thoughts, dreams new dreams, explore uncharted creative territory. What sort of creativity can the labyrinth foster? Walking the labyrinth can be used to:

- Ask for inspiration for a new poem, painting, hobby project
- Plan a festive meal
- Rehearse a presentation
- Create a new project proposal for work
- Practice brainstorming and creative problem solving
- Dream new dreams for your life, personally, vocationally, and spiritually
- Bring those dreams into reality

LABYRINTH AS GESTATOR

Everything is gestation and bringing forth," wrote poet Rainer Maria Rilke. "To let each impression . . . come to completion wholly in itself, in the dark, in the inexpressible, the unconscious, beyond the reach of one's own intelligence, and await with deep humility and patience the birth-hour of a new clarity: that alone is living the artist's life."

The labyrinth is the perfect "gestator" for creativity. Truly creative ideas emerge from deep within our hearts and souls, not from our everyday minds. Gestating a creative idea—just like gestating a child—requires a great deal of waiting and receptivity. The labyrinth can be womb for our own creativity; the more time we spend walking it, the more ideas and creativity will be birthed.

Intuitions and creative ideas are like evanescent bubbles rising up from deep within our souls. Even though they seem strong and present when we first receive them, they become increasing more difficult to access as we move back into our "regular" state of consciousness after leaving the labyrinth.

Get a small notebook and carry it with you during your labyrinth walks to record your ideas, thoughts, and inspirations. Look for a notebook or journal that easily opens flat and is convenient to write in without having to place it on a hard surface. If you like, you can even buy a notebook and decorate the cover.

I have a client who brings to her sessions a labyrinth notebook the cover of which she has decorated with a collage of inspiring magazine pictures. She walks the labyrinth after each session, recording new ideas that surface during her walk.

Ideas and inspiration can come thick and fast while you're walking, as you will discover. You can either bring your notebook with you and record as you walk, or keep your journal handy for writing immediately after the walk. I know someone who loops his spiral notebook on a string around his belt, so that he feels physically freer to walk than if he were carrying it. You can also walk directly to center and place your notebook there so that it awaits your arrival.

Whatever method you choose, remember how important it is to record thoughts, images, and impressions. I can't tell you how many times I have received a great idea while walking, and, sure I'd remember it simply because it was such a great idea or turn of phrase, didn't record it. When I tried to recall it several hours later, I would find to my chagrin that it had simply evaporated.

When you walk the labyrinth to foster creativity, the most important task is defining your intention. As mentioned before, we shape the quality of guidance we receive by the clarity of our intentions. What is it that you really need? What is your dream: A new painting? An office dilemma solved? New vocational or personal goals?

Clarifying your intention begins the gestation period, when we allow the project, idea, or dream to drop below our conscious awareness and "incubate," much as a mother hen incubates her eggs so that they may hatch. Walking the labyrinth is like mini-incubation: By engaging our bodies in outward movement, we are allowing the intention or question to drop deep into our psyches so that our souls may warm it and bring forth new life in response.

Take a moment now and think of what is currently your most creative challenge personally, relationally, vocationally, or spiritually. How would you best articulate what the challenge is? How would you articulate what the central desire or question is for you? When you've got your intention or question, walk to your labyrinth with your journal. Prepare in any way you'd like: light candles, breathe, stretch, anything that allows you to relax and be present.

State your intention or question at the entrance to the labyrinth, invoking if you wish any spiritual guidance. Begin walking, breathing and carrying your intention in your heart. Be open for images, intuitions, snatches of songs, feelings, and words, all of which may be responses to your intention or question.

Guidance often comes in sideways fashion. For instance, when writing a previous chapter I asked for help in not pushing so hard to get it done. Instead of receiving words or images, I heard a chant I hadn't thought of in years: "We are the flow/ We are the ebb/ We are the weaver/ We are the web." The chant stayed with me the rest of that afternoon and helped me remember to trust and enjoy the flow of the writing and not push.

Since creative intuition can be so ephemeral, note impressions as they come to you, even if they don't make sense at the time. The walk is not necessarily the time for making sense of creative guidance, though you may do so if it feels right and doesn't disengage you from your intuitive process. Otherwise, continue to breathe, walk, and remain open to the voice of intuition within you. When you get to the center, record any impressions if you haven't already done so. If you'd like, you can ask your wisest Self or Spirit, "How does this image, song, feeling, reveal guidance for my intention?" and begin journaling.

Another way to experiment with guidance when you reach the center is to write a letter from your wisest Self to your small self in response to your intention or question. Write quickly, without lifting pen from paper. Don't edit as you go or stop and think about what you're writing. The point, in any journaling designed to tap into your own guidance and intuition, is to get out of your own way. You can read and think about what you've written after you've finished writing.

GETTING THE JUICES TO FLOW

What if the creative juices don't flow once you've gestated an idea and are ready to begin the project? The blank canvas mocks you; you doodle with your pencil waiting for inspiration about that work project; you haven't a clue if plaid or paisley is the way to go in decorating your bedroom.

It happens to all of us at some point. It may be that the juices have temporarily dried up. Remember that there are cycles to everything, including creativity. The labyrinth has reminded me that sometimes I simply need to rest and be fallow. I also have discovered in the labyrinth that the juices aren't flowing sometimes because I haven't taken care of myself.

Once I was writing an article against a looming deadline, and all I could do when I sat down at the computer was stare at the blinking cursor on my screen. Finally I headed out to my labyrinth with the intention of unblocking my creativity, expecting to receive guidance on how to start writing again. Instead, at the center of the labyrinth a quiet voice asked me, "You're taking care of the story. Who is taking care of you?"

The question took me aback. I realized that I had been expending a lot of energy recently in other-care: child, clients, workshops. Everything and everyone, it seemed, except for me, had been cared for. I went upstairs in the middle of the afternoon and took a long fragrant bath.

I dried off, went back to my computer, and stared some more. *What now?* I thought. *Didn't I do what I was supposed to do?* I went out to the labyrinth and began walking with a tinge of self-righteous indignation.

Whoa, that voice said as I walked. *That was only one bath. Your energetic bank account is empty. How can you put out if there's almost nothing there?*

I had to take the rest of the day off, talking to my anxiety over the writing deadline as if it were a small child I needed to reassure. I took a long walk, went to my favorite bookstore, and made a commitment to myself to better self-care in the next month. I took another bath that night, went to bed early, and slept long and deeply.

The next morning I got up and wrote.

If you're feeling stuck, walk the labyrinth with the question, "Why am I blocked right now?" Put aside any preconceived notions about why, and open your heart and mind to what comes through. Remember to take your journal with you; you may receive some information that is challenging or surprising, and easy to "forget."

Others questions to walk with when blocked:

- What in my life needs to change in order to keep the creative juices flowing?
- How can I honor my own creativity more?

Walking the labyrinth with the intention to learn more about blocked creativity, and walking to allow your creative juices to flow more freely, is like inviting a divine Roto Rooter into your soul. Be prepared for the pipeline to open up!

AFFIRMATIONS

Working with affirmations is a powerful way to foster creativity. Most of us grow up with limiting beliefs about our creativity. Affirmations can introduce new information into an outdated and too-small belief system about our own capacities and gifts. Walking with affirmations in the labyrinth is also a very quick way to discover what your own internal destructive beliefs are about your own creativity.

You can walk with an affirmation as you would with a question or intention, repeating it in your heart as you walk. Sample affirmations that might get your creative/intuitive juices flowing are:

- I welcome my full creative powers.
- I am an open channel for creativity to flow through.
- Creativity brings me joy and life.
- My creativity blesses me and all those I love.

Walking with an affirmation can quickly flush out whatever is blocking your creativity. If an objection comes up to your affirmation, you can either note the objection gently, breathe into it, and let it go, or turn your attention to the objection if it has enough charge for you.

Let's say you need to plan an important report for work, one that will get you noticed for its innovative ideas. You sit down to begin the report several times, only to find that your mind zooms off elsewhere and you can't bring it back. Realizing that you're feeling anxious about the report, you go out to your labyrinth and begin walking with the affirmation "I allow my creativity to flow into this project."

Immediately a strong internal objection surfaces: "I can't!" Take a deep breath, keep walking, and ask yourself, "Why can't I?" A memory comes to mind: You're in fifth grade and about to give an oral report you've worked hard on for a month. You're excited, but nervous too. You open your mouth to begin but nothing comes out. Kids laugh. You want to die. Your teacher tells you to sit down and try another time.

As you relive this memory, you realize that part of you is terrified to go through with this report, even if—or perhaps because—it's so exciting to you. Keep walking, and keep breathing. As you walk, breathe into the humiliation and disappointment from long ago, and ask for healing. Once in the center, take some time to acknowledge that child's hurt and send light or healing energy his or her way.

On the way out, return to present time and to your affirmation. Chances are the affirmation will feel different, and you will be far more receptive to it.

I am currently working with a very powerful affirmation from *A Visionary Life*, by Marc Allen: "In an easy and relaxed manner, in a healthy and positive way, in its own perfect time." This affirmation directly challenges old beliefs about creativity being a struggle. As I walk with this affirmation in the labyrinth, my body and soul learn about relaxing into and trusting the creative process. I could work with the affirmation without using the labyrinth, but the labyrinth adds power and focus to the healing that the affirmation brings: When I walk with the affirmation, I am far more open to its meaning than I would be if I simply repeated it to myself elsewhere. The affirmation can work at a deeper level when I walk into it with my heart and soul.

Take whatever affirmation you create and walk with, and make a copy to put on your desk so you can see it frequently. I like to make a "sticky" of my current affirmation and place it on the computer's desktop.

DREAMING NEW DREAMS

Our blocks to our creativity are also blocks to our ability to dream wonderful dreams for our lives and bring those dreams into reality. Most of us not only feel that we can't open to our full creativity; we also feel that we can't allow ourselves really to envision what we want for our lives, our relationships, our work. Our life itself is the ultimate creative act. The greatest creativity we can manifest is co-creating, with Spirit, the dreams of our lives into physical reality.

The labyrinth is a wonderful place to begin envisioning how we want our lives and loves to unfold. It affords us time, and sacred space, to dream our High Dreams for our own lives. Sandra Sarr, the managing editor for Grace Cathedral's labyrinth newsletter *The Source*, began working with the labyrinth after she learned she had breast cancer. She asked herself as she walked, "I need to know, what is truly important to me? What am I doing here? What's my life purpose? Facing the potential end of my life motivated me to ask those questions and seek answers in a far more focused way than in my previous thirty-eight years of living. Life is a creative journey. We can just let life happen to us, or we can fully participate as co-creators with Spirit. The question is, what kind of life do I want? I have the capacity to shape my experience of life. And I know that I do not do it alone."

The labyrinth is where—free from old self-definitions of what we have been or pressures of what we should be—we can allow the flowering of who we're meant to be. Until we know what we dream for, yearn for, we can't work with Spirit to manifest it. We can walk in the labyrinth with such intentions as:

- What is my high dream for my life, my heart's desire?
- If I won the lottery and money and time were no longer issues, what would I do that would bring me joy, creative fulfillment, life?

Walking in this manner need not be reserved for the "big dreams." You can walk the labyrinth for help in envisioning a new job, a new work project, a new house—whatever it is that will allow you to live life more fully and abundantly.

Once you've figured out what you want, from something as mundane as how you'd like your next apartment to look, to something as grand as a soul mate or spiritual path, you can use the labyrinth, as Neal Harris calls it, as a "playground of the Spirit" to help manifest your heart's desire.

Manifesting in this way is not an act of will or "forcing" the universe to give you what you want. It is about attuning to your dreams, getting out of your own way, and allowing the energy of your clarity to help manifest your dream if it is for your own highest good.

The manifestation walk helps put your body and soul in alignment with your vision in a powerful way. Find a place to be quiet and center in. Close your eyes, take several deep breaths, and ask for a symbol of your heart's desire. When you receive the symbol, draw it or simply write the word for it on a slip of paper. Then go out to your labyrinth and place the symbol in the center.

Return to the entrance and ask for help in symbolically attaining your goal and becoming aware of whatever hinders you, internally or externally, from reaching that goal. Walk mindfully toward the center, staying aware of how it feels, body and soul, to walk toward your goal. As you walk, notice what feelings surface: excitement? anxiety? anger? fear? relief? joy? Breathe into each one, acknowledging it, and continue your walk. If a feeling feels "big," stop for a moment and breathe into it. Let yourself really feel it; move to it if you wish: Skip for joy, crouch in fear.

Let your body and soul direct you in how you get to the center and to your dream. Don't reach the center until you're really ready to embrace your dream. Once in the center, pick up your symbol. Look at it; breathe into it. Imagine bringing the symbol, and your dream, into your heart. Welcome it into your life. Stay with this until you feel as if you now carry this symbol in your heart. Notice how you carry yourself differently with the symbol inside you.

When the symbol feels integrated, you can either leave the piece of paper at the center of the labyrinth as an altar offering, or carry it out with you. Now walk out from the center. Imagine walking into your own life with this dream come true, as if it had already happened. Notice how you walk differently with this dream now a reality.

WALKING INTO A COMMITMENT

Another way to work with your heart's desire is to make a commitment to it. "Until one is committed, there is hesitancy, always ineffectiveness," the German poet Goethe once wrote. "The moment one definitely commits oneself, then Providence moves, too. A whole stream of events issues from the decision, raising in one's favor all manner of unforeseen incidents and meetings and material assistance."

Commitment to a dream opens doors that otherwise might remain shut. Commitment to a dream or a goal, just as in commitment to an intimate relationship, allows depths to unfold and synchronicities to occur. Often life begins to move dreamward only after a firm heart commitment has been made.

Making a commitment to a dream will flush out any inner blocks to its realization so that you can deal with them consciously rather than have them drive you at an unconscious level. You can use the labyrinth as a way of affirming your commitment to your heart's desire and releasing any internal roadblocks you carry to realizing your dreams.

To begin the "commitment walk," first take some time to reflect on what you are committing to, and why. Explore how realizing this dream will not only make you a better person but help others around you as well. When you are ready, stand at the entrance to the labyrinth and ask for help in making a heart commitment to your dream. As you walk toward the center, imagine walking with your dream. Notice feelings, images, thoughts that arise as you walk. Breathe through them all.

When you reach the center, commit either out loud or in silence to your dream. Make it clear what you're committing to, and why. Feel the depth of commitment in your body and soul. Walk out in celebration.

Occasionally the internal flutters you feel on walking into a commitment may turn into earthquakes. If you are being shaken as you walk with a tide of objections, stop walking. When serious internal resistance comes up to making a commitment, it's necessary to discern whether those objections are about fears and anxieties that need to be honored and worked with before making the commitment or whether the resistance is information about the necessity of changing your dream.

If you're not sure which way your resistance is directing you, you can simply finish the walk asking for discernment. If you discover that your dream needs to be modified to fit you better, walk the labyrinth for help in figuring out how to do that.

If you find that your dream is still true but your internal resistance needs to be dealt with, walk with your resistance, your fear, your anxiety. Notice where you carry it as you walk to the center. Ask it if it has any gifts for you. Discover how the resistance has been, in some way, an ally for you. Walk into your own heart, finding some way that this obstacle has been a blessing for you, something you can be grateful for.

When you reach the center, name the obstacle. Thank the obstacle for its gift or blessing. Then release it, surrendering it to Spirit. You can even make some gesture of release: Imagine throwing the obstacle into the air to be carried away by angels; reach down, touch the earth, and imagine sending its energy deep into the ground to be recycled. Thank Spirit for helping you release it and for carrying it away.

Walk out of the labyrinth feeling the weight of this obstacle gone.

Be aware that although the labyrinth is very powerful, it is not magic. Some obstacles may indeed be released in one walk. Others, particularly ones we have carried for a very long time, may need to be walked with many times, and surrendered many times, at the center before they are truly released from your heart and soul.

The more we can foster both creativity and intuition in the labyrinth, the freer we shall be to inhabit our highest and finest dreams for our lives.

CHAPTER TEN

Healing the Heart, Healing the Soul

Andrea came to me in the midst of a painful divorce and fearful of losing her job due to restructuring. She was angry, frightened, and confused. "I knew I needed help when I started and couldn't stop screaming at the kids," she told me when she began therapy.

Over a period of months she worked through her divorce and job loss issues. On the other side, with a new job and new life as a single parent, Andrea was ready to terminate therapy. I asked her what she had found most helpful in the work we did together.

"The labyrinth," she told me. "Therapy helped with my feelings, but the labyrinth healed me."

Andrea explained that walking my backyard labyrinth every week had given her a bigger context for her own life. "Each time I walked the labyrinth, I remembered that all the setbacks in my life were just twists and turns in my path. Really hard twists and turns, but not dead ends. I was always heading to center, even if it sure didn't look that way at the time. When I'd get to center, I'd remember a lot about those other twists and turns my life had taken—maybe not as challenging as divorce and unemployment, but still twists and turns. And in each of those, just like this last year, I felt like part of me and part of my life was dying. But in those other ones I kept on going, and, you know, new life came out of all of them, which was like reaching the center of the labyrinth.

"So I'd walk the labyrinth each week and remember all those other 'deaths' and the new life that came from them, and I'd realize that even out of all this mess could come new life. I just needed to keep putting one foot in front of the other and trusting that I'd reach that center.

"Remembering the bigger story of my life gave me courage and hope to keep on keeping on. I needed to walk each week, because I kept forgetting and would get really stuck in my feelings. Sometimes at the end of the day after putting my kids to bed I'd even close my eyes, when I was so tired and feeling so discouraged, and imagine walking the labyrinth.

"The labyrinth didn't solve my problems, but it healed my life."

Emotional pain can quickly bog us down in the overwhelming particulars of our story, making us contract around our pain in ways that preclude healing. Working with our suffering in the labyrinth invites us to open compassionately to our own pain, and allows that pain to be a threshold into new life. Many spiritual traditions view suffering—whether emotional, physical, spiritual—as an opening through which Spirit can pour its graces.

Walking the labyrinth is one of the most powerful yet simple ways to allow the light of healing to shine through, restoring our connection to Spirit, love, and life itself.

THE BIGGER STORY

The labyrinth is a great healer, a cosmological pathway that people have walked forever," says Linda Sewright, a labyrinth facilitator. She attributes the healing energies of the labyrinth to the fact that it opens us up, as it did Andrea, to the larger stories of life, death, and rebirth that people have been walking the labyrinth for ever since it was first used thousands of years ago. "When you walk the labyrinth, your story is part of a much larger picture, one filled with mystery; the labyrinth opens you to the mystery of your life and the greater mystery in which all life is held. This is what heals."

Seeing our life challenges as a journey into new life helps us walk into painful feelings as fires of transformation. These fires burn away the old and make room for new power and love and creativity, if we can allow the burning.

Toby Evans, the owner of the large Prairie Labyrinth made of native grasses, helps others walk the labyrinth as a way of opening more fully to their own story of life, death, and rebirth. She suggests making a paper copy of the labyrinth and fastening it to a piece of cardboard with glue or tape. Fasten a second piece of paper to the back side. Take this with you, along with a pencil or pen, as you walk. As insights occur to you about your own challenge as part of a larger life journey, note them directly on the paper labyrinth, at the same spot on the paper as you currently are on in the labyrinth.

When you reach the center, stop and meditate upon your journey. Turn the cardboard over and write a letter on the back from your larger, wiser Self to your smaller self about your life challenge and how it is a reflection of the Great Story. Ask your larger Self, "How is this walk like my own journey? What, or whom, in my life must I release? As I die to my old life, my old beliefs, my old self, what is asking to be birthed?" Let your larger Self give you a bigger perspective on how the particulars of your present life challenge fit into the Great Story of life, death, and rebirth.

SURRENDER

This opening into the greater story frees us to actively choose to surrender to, rather than resist, our experience in the present moment, trusting that there is always learning, and redemption, to be gained any situation.

Surrender does not mean giving up. Rather, surrendering to our pain, and our stories, while walking the labyrinth means no longer expending useless energy trying to control the outcome of a situation. By letting go of resistance to our own pain and to the reality of the situation that brings us grief, we open our hearts and souls to the healing power of Spirit and to creative ways to meet our life challenge with open hearts and clear eyes.

Resistance is like metaphorically closing our fists tight around the divorce, the bankruptcy, the job loss, the illness. Surrender means opening our hands so that the situation may rest lightly in our palms, allowing us to see it more clearly and also thus allowing the healing energy of Spirit to surround and fill it.

The first labyrinth at Harmony Hill was born out of executive director Gretchen Schodde's experience of surrendering to, rather than trying to control, her pain and confusion over her mother's cancer diagnosis.

Schodde went out to rototill her garden after learning her mother had cancer of the jaw. "I couldn't concentrate enough to take the rototiller back and forth in any kind of orderly way because I was so caught up in this situation with my mom that I was going in circles in my own head. The harder I tried to make the rototiller work, the worse it got.

"At some point, I think it was total grace, the absurdity of thinking I had to till in straight lines occurred to me, just because I had done it that way all my life. I actually started laughing and said to the rototiller, 'Okay, rototiller, I'm obviously incapable of controlling this right now, you take over.'

"What I was really doing was letting go of needing to control the whole painful situation with my mother. I remember this happiness at letting it all go, and started actually having fun because the rototiller started going in circles; I just held on and let it go where it wanted to go. It would go in a circle in one direction, and then I would nudge it a little and it would go in a circle in the other direction."

To her surprise, Schodde discovered a year later that what she called the Circle Garden was actually a labyrinth when she read an article about labyrinths that included pictures. Many years later, and thousands of walks—both hers and others'—later, Schodde recalls the huge impact letting go and surrendering had upon her pain and confusion over her mother's diagnosis. "The Circle Garden helped so much. The shifting of paradigms from straight lines to circles had a huge impact on me. I let go of all that struggle; creating the labyrinth helped me get a hold on my pain and stress in a way that was really life-giving."

This is the essence of surrender: acknowledging, and opening to, what is in our lives. This is an act of power we can make while walking the labyrinth: saying yes to our pain, our grief, our confusion. When we say yes, we are also saying yes to the possibilities of healing, and new life, emerging from the depths of that same pain.

GRIEF

Stephen Levine, author of many books on working with emotional and physical pain, calls grief the great softener of the heart. What happens for so many of us, though, is that grief seems so overwhelming that we close our hearts to our own grief, halting the healing process. Walking the labyrinth can reopen our hearts and allow the grief, and the healing, to flow.

If you are dealing with a loss, any loss, then walk the labyrinth. Walk into your grief. If you have lost someone you love through death or divorce, imagine walking with that person beside you in the labyrinth into the heart of your grief. Sit with him or her, and your grief, at the center. Ask your heart and soul if there is anything that has been left unsaid to this person. If so, say it.

Last year a close family friend died suddenly from a massive stroke. Killian had always been like a member of the family, a dear friend of my parents who had been a part of my growing up. I felt devastated when my mother told me he had died but was baffled by the depth of my grief until I realized that he had been like a second father to me. My grief deepened when I recognized that I could never tell him that realization in person, and thank him.

I took my grief and regret into the labyrinth. As I walked back and forth in the circuits on my way to the center, I relived memories of him chasing me and his daughters in childhood games. I heard his growly laugh and saw him beaming at me at my wedding. When I got to the center, I told him how much he had meant to me and cried. I told him how sorry I was that I had never thanked him for being in my life.

In the midst of the tears I felt my heart opening to an unexpected wave of gratitude for the gift of his presence throughout my life. It was as if I could hear him harrumphing in acknowledgment and acceptance of my love and gratitude. The tears ended and I walked out feeling profoundly grateful for his gruffness, his stability, his caring. Walking the labyrinth didn't "cure" my grief, but it allowed me to work with it in a powerful way. The labyrinth helped pull me out of regret and into gratitude for Killian's life and all he gave me.

You might find that walking the labyrinth unexpectedly brings up old residues of grief in order to be worked with and ultimately healed, as it did for Sig Lonegren, author of *Labyrinths: Ancient Myths and Modern Uses.* One year after his mother's death he traveled with a group to Chartres Cathedral in France. Other group members included a family consisting of an older woman whose first husband had died, her new husband, and her three grown children.

While Lonegren was walking the labyrinth at Chartres one evening, he recalled, "I began naming members of my own family; it was like I was doing a prayer for each one of them, totally unplanned. I looked into the center of the labyrinth and there was that woman on her knees bowing toward the altar with her kids gathering around crying for their dad, of course. All of a sudden she was my mother:

She was about the size of my mom and the color of her hair was like my mom's when she passed on. She *became* my mother. Her family suddenly became my family.

"It was an incredible release for me, a radically powerful experience. I was so touched that I sent my whole family a letter about what happened. Grief is so powerful. You think you've gotten over the loss, and three months later you're getting over it again. This walk was one of those very important 'getting over it' stages for me: thinking about my family, and saying their names, and praying for each one of them, and then seeing this woman become my mother in the center. It was a very powerful integration of my feelings about my mom and her death and all that meant for me."

Another way to open compassionately to your own grief is to imagine the labyrinth as the Open Heart of Spirit. Walk into this Open Heart; allow it to comfort you and surround you as you walk into its depths and graces. When you reach the center, listen to what this Open Heart has to say to you, teach you, comfort you.

I once had a client who was grieving the loss of her best friend due to an unfortunate misunderstanding. Her favorite way to walk the labyrinth was to imagine the labyrinth as her own heart and to walk slowly into it. "I've spent my whole life with plenty of room for everyone else, but no room for me, in my own heart. It's so hard sometimes to be compassionate toward myself, especially when I'm in pain. So when I imagine the labyrinth as my own heart, and walk into it and spend time at the center, I can know that there's plenty of space there for me, and I can soften toward my own life. And that changes everything, even the pain of the loss."

FEAR

*F*ear can be a great paralyzer. I can be gripped by fear—whether of the future, of an imagined upcoming trauma, of the terrible state of the planet—and know that being in that much fear is useless, yet I feel powerless to do anything about it. Those are times for walking the labyrinth. If you are feeling paralyzed by fear or worry, try the surrender walk.

As you stand at the entrance to the labyrinth, ask for help from Spirit in letting go of, or surrendering, your fear, and name that fear. Soften around the fear as you walk. Feel where you carry it in your body. Breathe into the spaces around the fear, letting it float.

When you reach the center, release your fear. Imagine reaching into your heart, or wherever in your body you feel the fear, and taking it out with your hands. Hold the fear up in your hands and let Spirit carry it away, or lean down and offer it to the earth, allowing the earth to take the fear and recycle its energy. Say—out loud or to yourself—"I release this fear. I open to the support and love of Spirit. I let that love and guidance fill me and surround me."

Listen for any guidance you may receive at this time. If you wish to, you can write it down. Walk out, feeling the absence of fear and the presence of Love. If you weren't able to totally release the fear, *imagine* what it might feel like to be without the fear. Notice how your body feels different, how you walk differently. Notice how releasing the fear changes how you think about the situation that triggered your fear and empowers you. If you received any guidance, breathe into that as you walk.

If the fear was a baby-size fear, one walk might be enough to release it. If the fear is more Goliath size, the releasing may take many walks and become a practice for you in a difficult time. The point is not about doing it right or perfectly; it is more like meditation, a conscious practice in turning the heart and soul toward Spirit in the midst of difficulty.

One client was struggling with a great deal of fear around an undiagnosed illness her small son was suffering from. Each week she returned to the labyrinth and surrendered her fear at the center. "Each week I would take it back," Elaine recalls. "However, the more I walked the labyrinth, the longer the lag time got between me releasing the fear and taking it back. It started reminding me of a small child giving a parent a broken toy, asking that the parent fix it. Well, the parent starts to fix it, but then the kid snatches it back. I started feeling like that little kid after a while—offering my fear up to my Higher Power but then snatching it back.

"After a lot of labyrinth walking I could start really trusting that my Higher Power could take my fear, if I could just really release it. When it would come back, when Jimmy and I were at the hospital with him undergoing more tests, sometimes when the fear would come up I'd just close my eyes and imagine releasing it, again, at the center of the labyrinth."

Her son Jimmy turned out to be fine. "I think about all the energy I saved from worrying from walking and releasing my fears about Jimmy's health," Elaine says. "Even if he had turned out to be seriously ill, saving all that energy from worrying would have given me a lot more coping resources to deal with it."

ANGER

Anger is another emotion that can paralyze, hardening the heart and blocking the possibilities for healing either within oneself or in a relationship. Walking the labyrinth when constricted in anger can soften your heart and often allow you to see the situation from the other person's viewpoint, releasing the tight grip around the certainty that we're 100 percent right and the other person 100 percent wrong.

Remember Mary Ellen Johnson and her friend, who walked the labyrinth together to resolve what then seemed like an unresolvable conflict? Both were able to release their "sides" and find common ground for healing the relationship.

If you are in conflict with someone, ask him or her to walk the labyrinth with you. Just agreeing to walk together can soften the conflict and allow room for healing. If the person won't walk with you, or if this is not possible, walk the labyrinth with him or her in spirit. As you walk, imagine how the person might be walking the labyrinth and seeing the conflict as the two of you walk together. Open your heart to the person as you walk together; allow for the possibility of healing.

As you walk, feel whatever hurt is underneath your anger. Moving to that level can allow for a softening of the heart and a healing that is not possible when the heart is hardened in anger and judgment.

My first response to feeling hurt by someone else is to harden in anger as a self-defense mechanism. I have learned to walk the labyrinth or use the finger labyrinth to center and soften before I talk with the other person about what triggered my anger. One morning, for instance, I felt let down by a colleague's treatment of me in a stressful teaching situation. My knee-jerk reaction was both anger and an old response of feeling victimized. I knew that if I went to her directly, I would act harshly and judgmentally.

I walked my backyard labyrinth first instead. As my breathing slowed and my heart softened, I allowed myself to walk the labyrinth metaphorically in her shoes. I let go of feeling victimized and could see the situation from her viewpoint. I could acknowledge, begrudgingly at first and more easily as I walked, that she was doing the best she could, and I could understand how she could also feel angry and misunderstood. After the walk I was able to talk with her from my heart rather than from an angry place of judgment.

Neal Harris teaches people in corporate settings to use a laminated paper finger labyrinth to deal with anger and frustration at work. He advises people to pull out their laminated labyrinth from their desk and trace it unobtrusively after dealing with an angry boss or a difficult client on the phone. "They can use it as a focusing tool. If the last caller was rude or frustrating, they might feel all over the place in their anger. Normally it might take them a while to get over the anger and get back to a center place where they can be more productive again.

"The finger labyrinth turns their attention both inward and toward the present moment, centering and relaxing them. They're much more capable of continuing their day without a lot of hoopla, instead of carrying their anger forward where they either have to keep talking about the last experience or taking it out on others around them."

The labyrinth, no matter what its size, provides a strong and safe container for the ups and downs of our emotional lives. When we walk through the sacred space of the labyrinth, we are reminded that all the twists and turns, the highs and lows, of our lives are sacred as well.

CHAPTER ELEVEN

Healing and Illness

Even if you or someone you love is not sick or in chronic pain, read this chapter. The great gift of physical illness is that it can be a powerful wake-up call to life. When I was seriously ill I was spurred on to ask the big questions: Why am I here? What, and whom, do I most value? What is my right relationship to Spirit? What is unlived in me—talents, gifts, experiences—that is asking to be birthed? How may I best live out the time remaining to me?

When you're facing serious illness, what is nonessential falls away. What surprises many of us, once we fall ill and take a thoughtful look at our lives, is how much time and energy we have expended on the things that are unimportant to the big picture. Serious illness and pain invite us to release false selves carefully crafted over a lifetime to please others and get ahead in the world. Facing our own mortality is a wake-up call to living from our authentic core.

Working in the Harmony Hill Cancer Retreat Program and in my private psychotherapy practice with people who are ill reminds me of how powerful a teacher pain and illness can be. It also helps me remember to keep learning the same lessons that I did when facing the possible end of my own life: not to take others, and life itself, for granted; to ask the big questions and be willing to wait and listen for the answers; to stay connected with Spirit, and my own soul, day by day, breath by breath.

All of us are learning these same lessons; it's just that with illness, the learning can be accelerated. The labyrinth can be a powerful ally in this learning, as you will discover in this chapter.

PHYSICAL HEALING AND CURING

The labyrinth is being used more and more frequently in hospitals, retreat centers, and private homes for healing from physical illnesses. "Healing" in this context does not mean "curing." A cure, as Michael Lerner writes in *Choices in Healing*, is "a successful medical treatment . . . that removes all evidence of the disease." Healing, on the other hand, "is an inner process through which a person becomes whole." Healing can happen at any level: physical, emotional, mental, or spiritual. Although healing and curing are deeply interconnected, "healing can take place on deeper levels whether or not physical recovery occurs."

The medical system's focus in our culture is too often concentrated on curing, fixing what is wrong with the body but forgetting that the illness occurs in the larger context of a human life and soul. In the medical model, "success" is connected solely with the physical outcome of disease or pain, a purely mechanical process. Healing is about attending to the wellness and the entirety of a person with an illness.

Ben, one of the participants at a Harmony Hill Cancer Retreat, explained to me his reasons for coming. "The first time the cancer came I went all out in getting the cancer cured," he told me in his elegant English accent. "I thought that was that. With the recurrence, I realize now that all my feelings, my heart, my soul had been left out the first time around. I want to pursue every medical option open to me, but I know that's about curing the cancer. I want something a lot deeper this time: I want healing."

The labyrinth is a powerful venue for healing from any illness or pain, whether the disease itself is cured or not. Walking with illness and pain can invite healing at the deepest levels possible, restoring right relationship with one's life, with God, with the past, with one's body, with relationships.

Sandra Sarr, editor of *The Source* newsletter, experienced healing with her breast cancer while walking the labyrinth. "I began to take the labyrinth seriously after surgery for breast cancer," Sarr recalls. "I first heard about the labyrinth when I was editor of *Science of Mind* magazine, but it was only after surgery that I was drawn to walk the labyrinth at Grace Cathedral as part of my healing journey. I was feeling so vulnerable. I had been so healthy, with a great career and family. Yet my body had seemed to turn against me. I was filled with fear, and feeling very much alone.

"I went into the labyrinth open for whatever would come into my awareness. I craved any connection I could find with Spirit. I was looking for support and help in releasing my fear. As I stepped into the twists and turns, I lost track of time and place. When I reached the center, I closed my eyes to connect with Spirit and let go of my fear. I asked for guidance and to feel Spirit's presence in a way that I could not deny. I asked for Spirit to give me courage and hope.

"When I opened my eyes they fell immediately upon the words in the stained-glass window above me, 'Light After Darkness.' The words weren't even connected on the window, but my eyes put them together from all the words interspersed on the window, 'Light After Darkness.' I just said thank you. I felt the deep gratitude of answered prayer for receiving the knowing that life would sustain me and not fail me.

"I needed that Light because I had just made a descent into darkness, not by choice but because of cancer. 'Light After Darkness' spoke directly to my situation and told me in no uncertain terms that there really was light after darkness for me. I don't know if I could ever adequately explain the power of those words I received in the labyrinth except to say that for the first time I felt, Sandy, you really are going to make it."

Sarr experienced healing in the labyrinth, as do countless others who walk for that purpose during pain and illness. The labyrinth supports healing in three primary ways:

- Promoting relaxation and destressing, allowing for tapping into one's own guidance about how to deal with the illness.
- Suspending of usual attitudes toward disease, disability, or pain, allowing reconnection to Self and Spirit.
- Inviting illness or pain to be an ally and teacher rather than a persecutor.

RELAXATION AND GUIDANCE

*A*t the most basic level, walking the labyrinth focuses the attention, stills the mind, and quiets the breathing. Once the mind is stilled and the heart opened—often quite a challenge in the midst of physical pain or life-threatening illness—the walker can tap into his or her own intuition and wisdom about choices to make about treatment and how to deal compassionately with the illness itself.

"Walking the labyrinth in our cancer retreat program is a healing force because it's about getting quiet," says Gretchen Schodde, a nurse practitioner as well as executive director of Harmony Hill. "The labyrinth is such a profound vehicle for grounding; walking the labyrinth nourishes these people step by step. The same thing happens with them that happened with me with the rototiller: realizing there's a way to the center, to stop going in circles so they can find purpose and meaning in the midst of their illness instead of feeling out of control.

"I know people feel so helpless, confused, and overwhelmed when they get into crises that involve the medical field. They often get so much information that they don't know how to deal with it, and the information is often conflicting. Walking the labyrinth gives people who are seriously ill a chance to find their own centers and sort things out, helping them to think through difficult decisions in a reflective way."

Neal Harris uses the labyrinth to work with those who are seriously ill. He theorizes that the design of the labyrinth is so ancient that walking it taps into the power of the collective unconscious. "Because people are following in the path, as they walk the labyrinth, of millions and millions of others who have trod it before them for healing and other higher purposes, all of that healing energy is available," Harris speculates. "It's not surprising at all to me that certain people tap into that wisdom and healing energy very profoundly, and it can provide them with guidance to troubling questions about their health.

"Because labyrinths have been used for healing at many levels over thousands of years, it's possible that that energy becomes tangible in the labyrinth. You dip yourself into this pool of energy and things happen, not physically like the pool at Lourdes, but at the level of transformation and healing."

Linda Sewright, a professional labyrinth facilitator, says that the healing power of the labyrinth stems from how it allows people to leave the cares and worries of their illness behind at the threshold of the labyrinth. "They can then open to something more than their usual way of looking at their illness, a larger picture than that afforded them by Western medicine. The labyrinth allows them to open to their own intuition and wisdom about their illness, which is always there underneath the worries."

When Sewright works with people with serious illnesses, "I talk to them about trusting the images they get while walking the labyrinth, and the messages they get." Sewright encourages them to leave their old selves at the threshold and ask while they're walking, "What if I were healed? What could the labyrinth say to me, offer to me, to do that? How could walking this path heal me?" She then encourages them to play with whatever comes in response as if it were real.

If you are ill, try walking the labyrinth asking these same questions. Perhaps you might walk before making any big decisions about treatment options. I also encourage seriously ill people to walk the labyrinth or use a finger labyrinth before visits to the doctor, to get clear on questions or concerns they may wish to present, and after the visit as well, to recenter and touch base with inner guidance on the visit and how to proceed.

RECONNECTION TO SELF AND SPIRIT

Walking the labyrinth affords a new perspective, allowing for new ways of seeing, and relating to, the illness itself. Mary Ellen Johnson, a Unity lay minister and labyrinth facilitator, remembers a woman suffering from arthritis who participated in a labyrinth workshop. "Walking was so difficult for her. Somewhere during the evening walk the pain just disappeared for her for quite a remarkable amount of time. She was able to soften and relax and just open up.

"I don't know how long after the workshop the relief continued, but it certainly opened the possibility in her thinking that she could have an effect upon her pain level, rather than feeling helpless or powerless. She was actually skipping around a lot as she came out of the labyrinth. It was remarkable."

I also have witnessed people with multiple sclerosis dancing gently through the turns of the labyrinth, normally a serious balance challenge for anyone with that disease. I have watched people with chronic pain moving with ease in ways they haven't for a very long time. Walking the labyrinth relaxes and softens us, allowing for pain to lessen, and also allows us to reconnect with a core self, unaffected by pain or disease.

When dealing with chronic or serious illness or pain, we can easily restrict our identity to our disease and our pain. Walking the labyrinth frees us up to find a deeper identity and the power that comes from that. "The greatest power we have is to be who we really are," says Robert Ferré, a labyrinth maker. "Our true nature, in the language of Christianity, is made in the image of God. The expression of that true nature is a powerful healing force. The labyrinth takes us back to our essential selves when we are ill; it unloads all our extra baggage. And a lot of that baggage is directly connected to our experience of our illness, because of the deep connections between mind and body."

Try walking the labyrinth to reconnect with your deeper Self, untouched by your illness. Imagine as you step into the labyrinth that you slip off your illness or pain for a moment. As you walk to the center, ask yourself, "Who am I if I am not this pain, this disease? Who is it that is beneath all this?" Imagine as you walk toward the center that you are walking into your essential Self, that deepest part of you that is unaffected by time, by pain, by illness.

Spend some time in the center, in your own center. From this standpoint, imagine looking back at the entrance, at the smaller you who is dealing with the suffering of illness. Walk toward that smaller you while asking yourself, "How does that smaller me get caught in the illness? How does that smaller me allow it to diminish me? What can that smaller self do to help me remember that I am not the illness or pain? How can my smaller self remember, and call upon, the larger vision and wisdom of my larger Self?" When you reach the entrance, welcome and embrace that smaller self, integrating both perspectives into your life.

ILLNESS AND PAIN AS TEACHER

Serious illness can be a profound invitation to living life more deeply and honestly. At cancer retreats, and in my own therapy work with people who are dealing with serious illness, people are surprised by the unexpected gifts that pain and serious illness can bring.

Sandra Sarr found that cancer sharpened her need to find her "heart's desires" in life. She used the labyrinth to explore the big questions, opening to guidance she received while walking: "I needed to know: What is truly important to me? What am I really doing here?

What's my life about? When you're facing the potential end of your life, believe me, you're much more motivated to ask these questions, and receive guidance on them, than you might otherwise be."

Make a list of all the Big Questions that pertain to your life, ones that you may have, as most of us have, put on the back burner while you went to work, raised kids, took vacations, watched TV. Ask questions like Sarr asked after she received her diagnosis.

After you have your list, take the questions one at a time into the labyrinth. Walk into the question just as you walked into earlier questions or intentions. Let go of the need to receive an immediate answer; the purpose of these questions is to open up space in your soul for deeper guidance to come through.

As you walk into the question, you may receive first glimmerings of answers or full-blown intuitions. Remember, the guidance may come in the form of images, feelings, sensations in your body, snippets of songs, and just plain knowings as well as verbal responses. Write them down, either as you walk or later; sometimes first knowings are ephemeral and hard to remember a day later, even if they are important.

In the midst of serious illness or chronic pain, it can be a challenge to see the illness and pain as anything but an affliction and enemy. Walking the labyrinth with the intention of seeing the suffering as a teacher can change the relationship, soften the suffering, and make room for gratitude, a healing force in itself.

I want to be very clear that walking to see the illness as teacher is not about being responsible in any way for the illness. Rather, it is about saying yes to all of one's life in a fundamental way, opening to the possibilities for healing and transformation inherent in any challenging life situation.

Real healing, someone once said, isn't about finding peace outside of the storm; it's about finding peace right in its center. Accepting your illness and pain as an ally and teacher, rather than something you have to push away or deny, opens the possibility for healing at a very deep level. By removing the sense of being at war inside of your body, you give your body the additional gift of peace, which can do nothing but boost your immune system and give you a greater chance of curing your disease.

Try walking the labyrinth into some of these questions:

- What is the most important lesson or lessons this illness or pain has taught me?
- In what ways am I more whole, healed, than I was before this illness?
- How has this illness spurred my search for meaning and wholeness?
- What in my disease or pain can I find to be grateful for?
- How can I continue to work with my illness as a teacher rather than as an adversary?

Adair, one of my psychotherapy clients, suffers from fibromyalgia, which brings with it significant chronic pain. She told me after one of her weekly walks in my backyard labyrinth, "I never wanted this illness or this pain; I wouldn't wish it on anyone. But walking into it in the labyrinth has taught me more about myself and living my life fully, from the center of my own soul, than any workshop I ever attended."

CHAPTER TWELVE

Ritual and Celebration

Marlene just finished her two-year graduate program. She gets her long hair highlighted and cut short.

Eloise, the day before kindergarten starts, decides to give up her cherished pacifiers and puts them away in a box she has decorated specifically for the occasion.

Rick's divorce just became official. He spends the afternoon going through his closet and drawers, taking out clothing he hasn't worn for a long time or that just seems too worn. With a great sigh of satisfaction, he loads the bags in his car and heads for Goodwill.

Pat just turned sixteen. New driver's license in hand, she picks up her best friend and they drive to the mall to celebrate.

Humans are hardwired for ritual. From time immemorial we have marked the power of transitions by enacting ritual. Tribal cultures commemorate birth, adolescence, marriage, priesthood, and death with elaborate and lengthy rituals in which the whole community participates.

Even in our sterile American culture we enact ritual to sacralize passages, because we must: The bar and bat mitzvah, the graduation ceremony, weddings, birthday parties, christenings, funerals, all carry vestiges of the numinous power of ritual. We unconsciously ritualize life transitions by cleaning out closets, cutting hair, going out to dinner, changing styles of clothing to mark on the outside what is at heart an internal transformation.

When consciously enacted, rituals bring all the power of Spirit to bear on life transitions great and small. Ritual, like sacred space, opens the threshold between matter and spirit, between inner and outer worlds. Tremendous healing and transformative energies are present during transition times in our own lives, in the seasons, in our relationships. Rituals focus and magnify those energies, not just for the one being celebrated but for all those present. Transitions, thresholds between the old and the new, become that much more powerful when marked with ritual.

Everyone has a different definition of ritual, but this is the working one I've devised from fifteen years of experience in creating rituals and rites of passage: A ritual is a series of symbolic actions carried out in sacred space and time for the purpose of transformation and healing.

The labyrinth, as sacred space, is a powerful container for ritual. For thousands of years the labyrinth has been used in rituals: funerals, fertility rites, initiations, blessings for voyages. Did you ever, as a child, use a magnifying glass on a sunny day to focus the sun's rays to burn a hole in a leaf? The labyrinth acts like a magnifying glass to further collect and focus the numinous and transformative energies of ritual.

Men and women around the country now are using the labyrinth's sacred space to:

- Celebrate weddings, birthdays, baptisms, and ordinations
- Conduct church services and healing rites
- Mark the passage from childhood to adolescence

- Mourn losses: loved ones, a stage of life such as parenthood, or an internal set of beliefs
- Welcome in a new stage of life, a new job, a new relationship or community
- Celebrate the passage of the seasons at solstices, equinoxes, and cross-quarters

"Since the labyrinth is sacred space, the power of ritual is enhanced there," says Sig Lonegren, who frequently conducts rituals in the labyrinth and celebrated his own relationship commitment ceremony there. "The function of sacred space, and the labyrinth, and ritual, is connection. Ritual in the labyrinth helps you make connection to whatever it is you're going for, whether that's healing or fertility or getting messages from Spirit."

THE STRUCTURE OF RITUAL

Once you understand the structure and function of ritual, you'll be able to create ritual in your labyrinth to mark transitions, from the mundane such as the daily transition between work and home, to the start or finish of a new project, to major life passages like the beginning and ending of relationships.

Ritual, just like any occurrence in life, has three stages: beginning, middle, and end. The beginning, or first stage, sets the scene: Participants are welcomed, the intention for the ritual is made clear, sacred space and time are delineated, Spirit is invoked. Just as in walking the labyrinth, a clear intention is absolutely necessary. I have attended far too many rituals that don't work simply because the participants have never clearly focused the purpose of the ritual. It was like aimlessly driving around in a car for several hours without a destination or a purpose, finally arriving back home. That is not ritual.

The second part, where one or a series of symbolic actions is carried out, is the heart of the ritual. These symbolic actions can be any number of things: burning, speaking, tearing. (See the list of symbolic actions at the end of this chapter.) These actions enact and embody transformation.

The third and final part is the closing: Spirit is thanked, the ending of sacred time and space is marked, the gathering is thanked and dismissed.

The next section includes guidelines to help you create a ritual to mark any life passage. If you haven't created ritual before, don't be intimidated. Most of us grow up with the idea of ritual as being something complex that someone else, an expert, "does." Let go of that notion. You have the power to create rituals that will greatly enhance any transition in your life.

As you read the rest of the chapter and the stories of rituals celebrated in the labyrinth, being to think about your own life. What transitions are you in or headed toward? What new beginnings, either at an inner level or an outer one, can be blessed? What endings can be grieved and released?

Start small and simple. Allow yourself to experiment. I tell "beginners" that Spirit joyfully welcomes and supports any attempt at sincere ritual. As you allow yourself to play with ritual, your confidence will grow as you experience the power of ritual to mark transitions and harness their enormous creative and transformative power.

After providing ritual guidelines, I'll take the rest of the chapter to describe several specific rituals that I and others have carried out in the labyrinth. If you get ideas while reading, jot them down. Then work with them with the listed guidelines.

RITUAL GUIDELINES

PREPARATION

- What is the purpose of my ritual? What do I want it to accomplish?
- Whom do I want to participate, and why? How much, or little, do I want them to do?

- How will the completion of this ritual affect my life?
- What symbolic actions do I want to carry out, such as burning, blessing, tearing, planting, cutting, burying, or washing?

ENACTMENT

Opening

- How will I consecrate sacred space and define its boundaries?
  ☐ decorating ☐ cleansing ☐ altering lighting
  ☐ music/music making ☐ seating arrangement ☐ incense
- How will I declare the intention of the ritual?
- How, if in any way, will others participate in the opening?
- How do I wish to invoke the Sacred?
  ☐ prayer ☐ words ☐ lighting a candle ☐ music
- What do I wish to ask from the Sacred?

Middle

- How will I carry out the symbolic actions?
- How, if in any way, will others take part?

Closing

- How will I end the ritual?
- How, if in any way, will others take part in the closing?
- How will I thank and release the energies that I have invoked?

INTEGRATION

- What did I learn from the ritual? How was I inspired by it?
- How can I continue to incorporate the gifts of the ritual into my life?
- What actions can I take to further ground the ritual in my life?

DAILY TRANSITIONS

Simple ritual in the labyrinth can mark beginnings and endings throughout the day, allowing you to be more open to the presence of Spirit in your life and more conscious of your intentions as you move through the day.

Gretchen Schodde and I created a ritual to begin the day we call "bringing in the Light" for dark Northwest winter mornings. When I am at Harmony Hill, Gretchen and I light candles at the entrance to the labyrinth, silently invoking Spirit in the darkness, and then light candles marking the four directions at the perimeter, inside the turns, and finally at the center, at the foot of the redwood tree. As I light the candles, I ask for Spirit to light my way throughout the day. I become clear about my intentions for that day, from specific (for example, to be fully present to participants at a retreat I am leading), to general (to remember to breathe, or let go and let God). Then I spend some time in the center in brief meditation and walk out.

Schodde, who lives at Harmony Hill, has incorporated the ritual into her daily wake-up routine throughout the long dark winters. "I first light a candle when I wake up in the dark, rather than turning on a light," says Schodde. "I then carry that candle out to the labyrinth. I have to walk much more slowly and meditatively than usual since I'm carrying the candle. I light the candles in the labyrinth, or just one in the center if I've got a lot to do. Lighting the candles is like blessing and thanking the labyrinth as a place that people can come to be restored and welcoming anyone who will show up that day to walk it.

"I then carry a candle from the labyrinth into my office and light a candle there before I turn on lights or computer. It reminds me about what's really important as I move into the workday. It also helps me hold an intention of keeping my life balanced between work and spirit, honoring what's important at the inner level so that it can create a proper foundation for my work at the outer level.

"I feel very honored to start each day this way, by connecting to the earth, the cycles of light and dark. I really notice the difference throughout the day between those mornings when I do the ritual and when I don't; my work stays so much lighter when I take the time to welcome in the light."

One couple I know, Mark and Alison each walk their labyrinth upon coming home from work to mark the transition between work time and family time. Mark tells me he goes over his workday, letting go of concerns and finding several things to be grateful for that happened during the day.

Alison uses the time to "change hats" from attorney to wife and mother. "The rules are so different between work and home," she says. "I use the walk to let go of the hard-driving, competent person I need to be in the office and soften into being in relationship once more with the people I love—my husband, my kids. Before I step into the labyrinth I ask for help from my Higher Power for softening and relaxing. I stay in the center until the 'hats' are really changed. Then, on the way out, I ask for blessings for the evening with my family."

Both Mark and Alison find that they can be much more present to each other, to their children, and to the graces of family life once they release their workday in the labyrinth.

Neal Harris advises corporate executives to do the same. After working with executives on stress reduction and centering in the workplace, he has them keep a laminated paper labyrinth in their desk. Before leaving work, he suggests that they pull out the labyrinth and "walk" it. "When you do that before you go home," Neal says, "you can leave all your 'stuff' at work. It's a way of taking good care of yourself, of destressing and relaxing. It's also a way of caring for your family, by leaving all the stresses of work at work."

LIFE TRANSITIONS

*A*merican culture is desperately poor in ways to mark transitions from one life stage to another, something tribal cultures know is vitally important, not just for the person in transition but for everyone else around them. Marking transitions such as puberty, menopause, or elderhood dignify the change, allow for the transformation to happen fully at all levels—physical, emotional, mental, and spiritual—and allow the community to recognize the one in transition as a new being, with new capacities, gifts, and responsibilities.

Our culture is particularly lacking, as many sociologists note, in marking the change from childhood to adolescence, perhaps the most important rite of passage in most tribal cultures. Using the labyrinth to mark and celebrate the change is a powerful way of recognizing a young man's or woman's shift from childhood to the beginning of young adulthood.

Thirteen-year-old Kyna, her mother, and their community integrated the labyrinth into a coming-of-age ritual I had the privilege to lead. Kyna used the labyrinth at the beginning and end of the ritual celebrating her first menstrual period.

Kyna, having walked the labyrinth many times before, walked it at the beginning of her ritual to signify the last walk of her childhood. After her mother had dressed her and blessed her, Kyna walked into the labyrinth and left a translucent blue glass egg, a symbol of her emerging womanhood, in the center.

During the women's circle for the central part of the ritual, we read poetry to Kyna, sang to her, and blessed her. During this time, Kyna showed us, and talked about, a small cornhusk doll, a symbol of her childhood. To conclude the ritual, Kyna walked the labyrinth once more. After meditating in the center on all she had experienced during the evening, she left the cornhusk doll in the center, and carried out with her the blue glass egg, her nascent womanhood.

You can use the labyrinth to mark any sort of life transition. Doing so in a birthday ritual can be powerful. On your next birthday, try this:

Stand at the entrance to the labyrinth. Light a candle, a special one you have picked out for this occasion, at the entrance—a birthday candle signifying you bringing your light into the world at birth. Ask for support and help for thinking about the previous year and previewing the next one.

As you walk toward the center, walk with the previous year. Think about the high points, the challenges. Ask your heart what important things you learned during the year, both through joy and through pain. As you walk you may have new insights, and feelings may come up. Breathe through them.

When you get to the center, sit and become quiet. Close your eyes, open your hands in your lap in a gesture of receiving, and ask Spirit for a birthday gift: a special word, image, phrase, or symbol to stay with you during the upcoming year. When you have received it, bring your hands up to your heart and place the gift there. Let your heart fully open to, and receive, the gift. Notice how it feels to be carrying this gift with you in your heart.

Walk out now, walking in your imagination into the next year of your life. Notice how carrying this gift in your heart and soul affects how you see the upcoming year. Back at the entrance to the labyrinth, see the light of your gift reflected in the light of the flame. Extinguish the candle, thanking Spirit for the gift.

Take the candle back with you to your bedroom, office, or altar or meditation space. Through the next year, when you are in particular need of your birthday gift, light the candle for a moment and feel its presence in your heart.

GRIEF AND LOSS

Ritual in the labyrinth can be a powerful way to bring healing and closure to the loss of a relationship or a life situation, such as a job. We have already looked at some ways to grieve in Chapter 11. Here is another way to mourn and let go. Allow at least one hour for this ritual.

To prepare, you will need paper (or your journal) and pencil, a clipboard on which to write, a Pyrex or other fireproof bowl, matches, and a glass of water (which will be for drinking and washing yourself clean, and also stand in an emergency for a fire extinguisher). Take all of those to the center of the labyrinth. The purpose of this ritual is to literally walk through the relationship in time (or the history of a job, or of living in a particular house), doing a walking retrospective of it from beginning to the present moment. When you reach the center, you will journal about what needs releasing in order to allow healing in. After writing, you will burn the paper in the center in a gesture of releasing. This will allow the paper, and what is being released, to transmute into new energy.

Stand at the entrance to the labyrinth. Ask for help in grieving, releasing, and healing the relationship or situation. When you are ready, remember the first time the two of you got together: a chance meeting, birth, blind date. Bring yourself fully back to that time: See it, hear it, smell it, touch it, feel it. When you are fully there, take your first step into the labyrinth.

With that first step, take a step forward in time from your first meeting. Begin walking very slowly through time into the relationship as you walk toward the center of the labyrinth. Allow everything to come up: memories, thoughts, feelings. When you hit an intense place in the walk through your relationship, stop. Cry, breathe, shake your fist at God or the other person. Open your heart to yourself and the unfolding of this relationship through time. Move through the good times, the bad times, the end of the relationship as you knew it. If you find yourself spacing out, stop, breathe, and ground. Send compassion to yourself. When you are ready, take up where you left off.

Allow as much time as you need to get to the center; do not arrive until you have reached the present moment of the relationship. Sit down and take a moment to meditate on the journey you just completed. If you have any fresh insights that you want to keep, write them down in your journal, to take out from the labyrinth with you.

Breathe, ground, and say another prayer if you wish for help with healing the relationship. Meditate on what it is you need to release, let go of, surrender, in order for the relationship, and your grief, to heal. As you become aware of what you want to release, write it down on paper you can later burn. Try writing with your nondominant hand; often this will give you access to unconscious thoughts and feelings that are more difficult to access with your dominant hand. (Don't worry about it being legible: Remember, this is to burn.) If you wish, you could also write a letter from your larger, wiser Self to your smaller self about what needs to be released for healing.

When you feel done (ask your body as well as your heart if you're finished for the purposes of this ritual; you should get a feeling of lightness or relief physically), take the pages out of your journal. Wad them up and place them in the burning bowl. As you light them, say out loud, "I release all of this, so that I may be healed." If you wish, you also can ask that the other person be healed as well through this burning.

As the paper burns, feel the release within you. When you are left with ashes, drink the water, imagining it washing your soul clean. Ask for love and healing to move into the places in your heart and soul left open by the ritual. If you wish, you can imagine this as light filling all those places.

Take all the time you need here. Journal if you wish. When you are ready, take the burning bowl in your hands. (Leave the glass and journal to retrieve later.) Walk out carrying the ashes with you. Stay present to whatever is happening inside you, and breathe through it. When you reach the entrance, thank Spirit for healing and release, and pray that the healing may continue.

After the ritual is over, you can either release the ashes under running water or bury them in your garden. Roses and lilacs thrive with ash amended to the soil, and I love the idea of ashes of the old fertilizing new life—both literally and metaphorically.

CELEBRATION/BLESSING

The labyrinth can be used to celebrate beginnings as well as to mourn endings. For this celebration ritual you will need a candle and a symbol of what is to be celebrated. For instance, if it is a new relationship or a birth, you can take into the labyrinth a picture of your loved one or baby. If it is a new job, take in the contract, or something that represents the particulars of your job. If it is school, take a textbook.

At the entrance to the labyrinth, light the candle in gratitude for this new light coming into your life. Ask Spirit to be with you in this ritual, blessing the new venture and guiding and supporting you through it.

Walk to the center of the labyrinth thoughtfully, holding the object before you with both hands. Treat it as if it were a sacred object, which it is. Acknowledge as you walk how this new beginning is bringing healing and transformation into your life. If you are also aware of challenges it is bringing in (and all new beginnings bring those as well!), acknowledge them and ask Spirit to bless them and to support you in learning the most from the challenges; ask that they unfold for your own and others' highest good.

When you get to the center of the labyrinth, hold the symbol up before you. Ask that Spirit bless this symbol. Imagine light pouring into the symbol and filling the venture with the grace and light of the Sacred. Feel that light and grace filling you as well.

You may either leave the symbol in the center of the labyrinth as an altar offering for a while or take it back out with you. When you reach the entrance, extinguish the candle, thanking Spirit for its blessing and acknowledging your gratitude once more for this new beginning. Take the candle back with you to burn whenever you need reminding of the graces of this new beginning or when you wish to have a moment of celebration and gratitude again.

I have used this ritual a lot for writing, taking book proposals and first chapters into the labyrinth for blessing. This ritual helps me remember, when I am in the "slogging" stages of writing, that this is a sacred venture, one that, I hope, brings new life and healing not just to myself but to others who will read my words. It helps me keep the bigger picture in mind when I have gotten lost in the details.

SEASONAL TRANSITIONS

The labyrinth can be used to mark transitions in the cycle of the seasons as well as personal transitions. Honoring Summer and Winter Solstice, Spring and Fall Equinox, in the labyrinth is important for two reasons. First, the ceremonial honorings reconnect us to the cycles of seasons, powerful rounds of birth, death, and rebirth, that seat us within the sacred cycles of the earth and of life itself. Second, because these are transition times in the great rounds of life, they can be powerful times for personal reflection and taking stock of life direction.

I love to mark Winter Solstice in the labyrinth. Living as far north as I do, the light becomes perilously transient as the winter deepens. Celebrating this solstice in the labyrinth is a way to remember that the Light, and new life, will return to the earth and our lives even in the midst of deepest darkness. It is also a powerful reminder of the light that we all carry within us, in hearts and souls and spirits, no matter how dark it is outside. Rituals center around lighting candles, releasing the old by speaking or burning that which is to be released, and inviting in new life, new relationships, new projects.

Spring Equinox is a time for both celebrating new life, and reflecting on balance, since this is one of the two times of the year when light and darkness are equally balanced. Rituals at this time involving the labyrinth can include planting bean seeds in paper cups in the center. Use broad flat beans such as fava beans, and write on each one something that is just starting in your life that you'd like to welcome into being or dreams you would like to "plant" in the upcoming year. Make your symbolic action be planting them in paper cups at the center of the labyrinth.

You can also do a ritual around reflecting on balance in your life, balance between self- and other care, between work and home, and so on. After reflecting in the center of the labyrinth, write down one commitment you can make for restoring balance in your life. Speak it out loud in the center, and ask Spirit to help you.

Summer Solstice is a time to celebrate the Light and life in its fullness. I love to decorate the labyrinth altar with wreaths of St.-John's-wort, a herb that breaks into gloriously sunny blossoms right at solstice. Like many other labyrinths, the redwood labyrinth at Harmony Hill is oriented so that the entrance faces exactly where the sun rises on Summer Solstice. Gretchen Schodde and others walk the labyrinth at Summer Solstice dawn—quite a feat for this far north, since solstice dawn occurs about 4:30 A.M.!—welcoming the day of the zenith of the Light.

Rituals for Summer Solstice center on gratitude for the Light around and within us all and celebrate the richness of life blossoming everywhere at the height of summer.

Autumn Equinox is once again a time to reflect on balance. It is also a time to celebrate that which has been harvested in the past year and to prepare to turn inward once more as the darkness deepens.

Rituals for Autumn Equinox can center on reflecting on balance, as in the Spring Equinox. You also can ritualize thanksgiving for what is coming to fruition and harvest in your life. Take symbols for these into the center of the labyrinth, and express gratitude to Spirit for the harvest, asking the continuing guidance of blessings of Spirit in further harvests.

You can create rituals for Autumn Equinox around acknowledging moving into the dark and inward time of the year. Take some time in the center to turn inward. What healing needs to be done at an inner level? What in your own personal shadow is asking for attention and healing? Reflect on these questions, and make a commitment to work with healing one specific inner wound. Speak that commitment out loud, and ask that all the healing energies of the spiritual world come to help you in this undertaking.

The opportunities for ritual and celebration in the labyrinth are endless. Sig Lonegren, author of *Labyrinths: Ancient Myths and Modern Uses,* celebrated his relationship commitment inside the labyrinth with his community gathered around. I once ordained a woman in the center of the Harmony Hill's garden labyrinth, in all its high summer glory of zinnias, basil, echinacea, and marigolds.

I walk the labyrinth both on the eve of my birthday, to contemplate the passing year, and on the day of my birthday, to celebrate and ask for guidance for the coming year. Others walk the labyrinth to honor the ancestors on the Day of the Dead, to celebrate in community the completion of a group project, to honor the coming of age of a young man or woman in the family.

How you use the labyrinth in ritual or celebration is limited only by your imagination and willingness to play and experiment. Ritual and celebration are powerful when thoughtfully planned and carried out. But also give yourself permission to play with spontaneous ritual and celebration.

The labyrinth is a container for life, life in all its glories and griefs, its heartaches and joys. The labyrinth welcomes all experiences into its circuits, teaching us to enter more deeply into the experience of life itself.

I have walked the labyrinth for many years now. My relationship with this powerful tool and archetype of wholeness and transformation reminds me in many ways of a relationship with a beloved other.

The mysteries and spirit of the labyrinth seem only to deepen with time. The more I walk its circuits, the more I realize I have barely begun to fathom its depths.

What the labyrinth has taught me, more than anything else, is the gracious power of process. Each time we step into its circuits, we step into the unknown, just as we do each morning when our bare feet first touch the cold floor. Walking the labyrinth has taught me to walk my own life more consciously, with more trust for the unfolding, knowing that I am always moving toward the center.

My hope for you is that your journey, both through the labyrinth and in your life, will be equally graced.

Gratitude Walk

I light a white candle at the entrance to my favorite labyrinth in this misty Northwest predawn. Other candles flicker around the perimeter and in the center, creating circles of fire in the darkness. Before taking the first step onto the labyrinth's gravel path I pause and say a brief prayer, as I have done so many times before.

As I walk the winding circuits in the growing light I feel the coastal mist on my face, listen to the crunch of gravel beneath my feet, and settle into the rhythm of step upon step, inbreath and foggy out-breath. I am walking in the light on this cold December morning, participating with earth and sky in the re-creation of the world, the birthing of a new day.

My breath catches and I halt at an unfamiliar faint sound. I listen carefully but hear nothing save the soft sighing of wind in the long limbs of the redwood tree at the center of this labyrinth. I take another step and stop. There *is* something, or someone, here with me.

Curious, I look around. I see no other creatures.

I begin to walk again and realize that the presence, or presences, I am sensing are unseeable. Other labyrinth pilgrims are here walking these circuits beside me in the gray and growing light. They journey with me, all those who have trod this winding path for almost four thousand years, pacing labyrinths of wood or turf or stone, on deserted moors and in Gothic cathedrals, on wild and rocky coasts and in hot desert sand.

The crunch of my sneakers on gravel is all that I now hear. I stop once more and bow in deep gratitude to all those who have walked the labyrinth before me. Taking a deep, frosty breath, I continue on, celebrating that others have walked, and will continue to walk, this sacred path.

Annotated Bibliography

Artress, Lauren. *Walking a Sacred Path: Rediscovering the Labyrinth as a Spiritual Tool.* New York: Riverhead, 1995.

Artress's engaging story of "rediscovering" the Chartres labyrinth and spearheading much of the labyrinth renaissance. *Walking a Sacred Path* is an in-depth look at the Chartres labyrinth as a spiritual tool, containing Artress's and others' stories of walking the labyrinth for emotional healing and spiritual growth.

Fisher, Adrian, and Howard Loxton. *Secrets of the Maze.* London: Thames & Hudson, 1997.

Engaging oversize book devoted to overview of mazes and labyrinths using many visuals. Traces the history of mazes and labyrinths from antiquity to contemporary innovations.

Jaskolski, Helmut. *The Labyrinth: Symbol of Fear, Rebirth, and Liberation.* Boston: Shambala, 1997.

History of the labyrinth, using the myth of Theseus and the Minotaur as an archetypal frame. Scholarly and heavily philosophical book translated from the German.

Kern, Hermann. *Labyrinthe: Erscheinungsformen und Deutungen 5000 Jahre Gegenwart eines Urbilds.* Munich: Prestel-Verlag, 1982.
Impressive German tome, the most exhaustive historical treatment of labyrinths available, replete with pictures and graphics. Available through Caerdroia and One Heart, which is currently undertaking the massive project of translating the book into English.

Lonegren, Sig. *Labyrinths: Ancient Myths and Modern Uses*, 2nd ed. Glastonbury, England: Gothic Image Publications, 1996.
Pioneering book on labyrinths containing the author's speculations on their origins and meaning. Explains a novel and powerful way to walk the Cretan labyrinth integrating the chakra system.

Matthews, W. H. *Mazes and Labyrinths: Their History and Development.* New York: Dover, 1970 (reprint of British work from 1922).
Scholarly look at mazes and labyrinths throughout European history. Excellent drawings of various forms of labyrinths.

Purce, Jill. *The Mystic Spiral: Journey of the Soul.* New York: Thames and Hudson, 1980.
Fascinating exploration of the spiral as it appears in nature, science, art, and religion. Many black-and-white and color illustrations.

VIDEO

Mazes and Labyrinths: The Search for the Center.
Produced by Scott Campbell. Winner of the CINE Golden Eagle Award. Thirty minutes, VHS. Available through Lutz Limited, P.O. Box 13926, Scottsdale, AZ, 85267-3926.

APPENDIX

Labyrinth Resources

LABYRINTH INSTRUCTIONS, KITS, AND PORTABLE LABYRINTHS

A-MAZING LABYRINTH KIT

2332 Senita Drive, Lake Havasu City, AZ 86403. Tel: (602) 680-9513. Labyrinth instruction kits.

RELAX FOR LIFE

Neal Harris. 26402 Edgemont Lane, Barrington, IL 60010. Tel: (847) 842-1752. E-mail: Relax4Life@aol.com; website: www.relax4life.com. Labyrinth kits for Chartres labyrinth and eight-walled Roman labyrinth. Cretan and Chartres wooden finger labyrinths.

ST. LOUIS LABYRINTH PROJECT

Robert Ferré. 128 Slocum Avenue, St. Louis, MO 63119. Tel: (800) 873-9873. E-mail: robert@1heart.com; website:

www.1heart.com/labyrinth.html. Canvas labyrinths; rope labyrinth kits; instructions for both Cretan and Chartres labyrinth construction, including instructions on how to adapt a Chartres labyrinth to a room with pillars. Canvas Chartres labyrinth. Paper Chartres labyrinths available in several sizes.

VERIDITAS

1100 California Street, San Francisco, CA 94108. Tel: (415) 749-6356. website: www.gracecathedral.org/veriditas. Instructions for creating Chartres labyrinth. Canvas Chartres labyrinth. Wooden finger labyrinths. Decorative labyrinths made from slate or glass that may also be "walked."

VOICES OF THE LABYRINTH

Alex Champion. PO Box 145, Philo, CA 95466. Tel: (707) 895-3375. E-mail: champion@zapcom.net; website: www.earth-symbols.com. Instructions for creating both Cretan and Chartres labyrinths.

LABYRINTH BUILDERS/CONSULTANTS/LECTURERS

Lauren Artress, c/o Verditas, 1100 California Street, San Francisco, CA 94108. Tel: (415) 749-6356.

Alex Champion, PO Box 145, Philo, CA 95466. Tel: (707) 895-3375. E-mail: champion@zapcom.net.

Robert Ferré, 3124 Gurney Avenue, St. Louis, MO 63116. Tel: (800) 873-9873. E-mail: robert@1heart.com.

Neal Harris, 26402 Edgemont Lane, Barrington, IL 60010. Tel: (847) 842-1752. E-mail: Relax4Life@aol.com.

Sig Lonegren, PO Box 218, Greensboro, VT 05841.
Tel: (802) 533-2240. E-mail: sig@geomancy.org.

Annette Reynolds, 205 Oak Road, Birmingham, AL 35216.
Tel: (205) 979-1744. E-mail: AnetRey@aol.com.

Melissa West, c/o Harmony Hill, 7362 East Highway 106,
Union, WA 98592. Tel: (206) 427-1325. E-mail: triplespiral@earth-link.net.

LABYRINTH ORGANIZATIONS

CAERDROIA
53 Thundersley Grove, Thundersley, Benfleet, Essex SS7 3EB,
England. Tel: 44 01268 751915. E-mail: Caerdroia@dial.pipex.
com; Website: http://ilc.tsms.soton.ac.uk/caerdroia. Nonprofit
organization founded in 1980 to provide focus for study of
mazes and labyrinths. Produces annual journal, supports ongoing research programs and networking among enthusiasts and
professionals, and supports preservation and restoration of historical labyrinths and mazes.

VERIDITAS: THE WORLDWIDE LABYRINTH PROJECT
1100 California Street, San Francisco, CA 94108. Tel: (415)
749-6356. Website: www.gracecathedral.org/veriditas. Nonprofit organization publishes a quarterly journal, *The Source*.
Provides training for labyrinth facilitators.

LABYRINTH PRODUCTS

FOREST OF PEACE
Tel: (800) 659-3227. Website: www.forestofpeace.com/
sacred_art/labyrinth/index_labyrinth.html. Pewter labyrinth
pendant. Etched stone labyrinth.

LABYRINTHINA

PO Box 14033, North Palm Beach, FL 33408. Tel: (561) 776-6050. Ocarina labyrinth flute necklaces.

VERIDITAS

1100 California Street, San Francisco, CA 94108. Tel: (415) 749-6356. Website:www.gracecathedral.org/veriditas. Glass coffee mugs, postcards and posters, silver and pewter pendants. Music to walk labyrinths by.

VOICES OF THE LABYRINTH

Alex Champion. P.O. Box 145, Philo, CA 95466. Tel: (707) 895-3375. E-mail: champion@zapcom.net. Labyrinth T-shirts, pins, articles, books.

FINGER LABYRINTHS ON THE INTERNET

These labyrinths can be "walked" directly on your computer screen, or you can download and print the images.

Cretan labyrinths: www.geocities.com/Yosemite/6182/labig1. html and www.mindspring.com/~daniel12/labyrinth.html.

Video and Shockwave demonstrations of how to draw a Cretan labyrinth: www.mcli.dist.maricopa.edu/smc/labyrinth/activities. html.

Animation of drawing of Cretan seed pattern: www.geomancy. org/home.html.

Chartres labyrinth: www.cl.ais.net/jhermann/uuce/labyrinth/ index.html.

Index